D1832414

TOURISM, BIODIVERSITY AND SUSTAINABLE DEVELOPMENT

(In 6 Volumes)

Concepts Definitions and Classification of Tourism

(Volume 1)

Editor

Prof. O.P. KANDARI

ASHISH CHANDRA

ISHA BOOKS

DELHI—110 033

Tourism, Biodiversity and Sustainable Development
(Tourism/Culture)

Rs. 5000 (Set in 6 Vols.)
Rs. 850 (Each Volume)

© O.P. Kandari; Ashish Chandra

ISBN: 81-8205-033-2 (Set)
ISBN: 81-8205-034-0 (Vol. 1)

All rights reserved. No part of this book may be reproduced in any manner without written permission.

Published in 2004 in India by
Isha Books, D-43, Prithviraj Road
Adarsh Nagar, Delhi-110 033

Lasertypesetting by: Varsha Graphics, Delhi
Printed at: Chawla Offset Press, Delhi

Preface

Tourism can be defined as the activities of persons travelling to and staying in one place outside their usual environment for not more than one consecutive year for leisure, business and other purposes. It is a comprehensive and extensive phenomenon. It is made up of various sectors or sub-industries such as transportation, accommodation, attractions, amenities, catering, entertainment, eating and drinking establishments, shops, activity facilities, and many others. It generates physical and financial flows that have strong economic, socio-cultural and environmental impacts. To study the domain of tourism one must quantify and interrelate the various characteristics of tourism.

The tourism sector has been characterised by two distinct operational paradigms since the post-war period, namely, mass tourism and the new age of tourism. Mass tourism was the logical outcome of prevailing economic and social influences. Imitating mass production in the manufacturing sector, mass tourism became the industry's best practice. The new age of tourism developed due to the inability of mass tourism to respond adequately to the changes that occurred in the industry in the 1980s. These changes can be grouped into a number of categories, specifically: new consumers, new technologies, new frame conditions, new forms of production and new management styles.

New management techniques and production practices serve to facilitate the development of the new services, whilst new frame conditions influence the speed and direction of these transformations. The tourism industry has thus entered a new phase, sometimes labelled a new paradigm. In this new environment, the demands of the new consumer will be the driving force of future competitiveness. It will also be vitally important that the tourism industry embraces all new forms of information and communications technology.

The book is not a simple compendium of facts and figures. Instead, it is a balance of much-needed concepts associated with the analysis of tourism. It suggests that today's information societies already possess a valuable tool box of instruments and policy options for steering tourism on a more sustainable path, while recognising that good governance requires political will, a sense for choosing the 'right scenario', international partnerships and an increased understanding of the complex cultural and ecological consequences of tourism.

Editor

Contents

1

Concepts of Tourism

Tourism is such a diverse phenomenon that a single social theory may not be able to explain. It is voluntary, outside ordinary life, limited in time and space, surrounded by an air of mystery, utterly absorbing yet recognized as as being somewhat makebelieve, has something at stake, an outcome in doubt and may promote the formation of social groups. No single theory has emerged which has been universally accepted by tourists researchers.

Search for the Authentic: The tourist wants to find what is real, pure, good or meaningful in the world; it represents the quest for the authentic.

Form of Play: It is assumed that humans have the need to process information. When a person is faced with a stimulus where he or she is unable to predict the outcome of the event, a conflict is created which promotes the processing of information to reduce uncertainty. Exploration is encouraged when the event has many things which can be seen, heard, touched, smelled, tasted or manipulated.

Imperialism: Some view tourism as a process by which one group comes to dominate the other. Tourism represents an expansion of a society's interests abroad which are imposed upon or adopted by the guest culture. When tourism occurs between individuals from technological inferior and superior cultures there is a cycle which leads to imperialism.

There is no agreed upon definition of tourism. The term may refer to anyone who travels or it may specify reasons for travelling such as sightseeing, visiting friends, educational or cultural trips, participating as visitors at special events, shopping expeditions, rest and relaxation or others. Tourism professionals may consider it tourism only if there is an overnight stay or if the destination of travel is more than a specified distance from the traveler's home, such as fifty miles. Generally, there is also the implication that such travel is not part of a daily routine.

Definition of "international tourism" was recommended by Council of Nations' League; in 1953 it was adjusted by Statistics Commission of United Nations, which admitted definition of "international visitor". 1967 m. this commission ratified definitions of "visitor", "tourist" and "excursionist". In 1993, Statistics Commission of United Nations in its 27th session ratified "Tourism statistics recommendations", which were prepared by World Tourism Organization. Tourism forms and categories, descriptions of the main tourism definitions, tourism supply and demand classification, Standards of International Classification of tourism activity (SICTA) were described in it.

Primal definition "traveler" is described as "any person who travels from one place to another irrespective of trip's purpose and kind of transport. "Visitor" is "any person who travels to another place outside his/her usual environment for a period not exceeding 12 months and whose main purpose of visit is other than the exercise of an activity remunerated from within the place visited".

According to forms of tourism visitors are divided into international visitors and domestic visitors. According to duration of a visit – to same-day visitors and tourists (visitors who stay at least one night in a collective or private accommodation establishment in the country visited).

Forms and Categories of Tourism

In relation to a given country, the following forms of tourism can be distinguished:

— *Domestic tourism,* involving residents of the given country travelling only within this country;

— *Inbound tourism,* involving non-residents travelling in the given country;

— *Outbound tourism,* involving residents travelling in another country.

These three basic forms of tourism can be combined in various ways to derive the following categories of tourism:

— Internal tourism, which comprises domestic tourism and inbound tourism;

— National tourism, which comprises domestic tourism and outbound tourism;

— International tourism, which consists of inbound tourism and outbound.

Tourism is the activities of persons travelling to and staying in places outside their usual environment for not more than one consecutive year for leisure, business and other purposes. There are three elementary forms of tourism in relation to a given area (e.g. region, country, group of countries) :

i) *Domestic tourism:* This is defined as comprising the activities of residents of a given area travelling only within that area, but outside their usual environment;

ii) *Inbound tourism.* This is defined as comprising the activities of non-residents travelling in a given area that is outside their usual environment;

iii) *Outbound tourism.* This is defined as comprising the activities of residents of a given area travelling to and staying in places outside that area.

Tourism is a comprehensive and extensive phenomenon. Tourism is demand led and influenced by many external factors. It generates physical and financial flows that have strong economic, socio-cultural and environmental impacts. To study the domain of tourism one must quantify and interrelate the various characteristics of tourism. In practice most tourism statistics take the transactors in the tourism process as their starting point, in particular visitors and direct supplier. Factors influencing tourism, the impact of tourism and the interrelation between supply and demand are usually tackled by integrating data from a great number of sources followed by model type analysis.

Tourism: Different Definitions

In recent years, increasing attention has been paid to the management and marketing of tourism, hospitality, and leisure, which have been widely recognized as very important sectors of the service economy. However, a different approach to the management and marketing of tourism, hospitality, and leisure services than to that of physical goods is required.

Tourism has a number of different definitions. It is very difficult to pinpoint a definition that would give a meaningful and adequate explanation of tourism, because the concept is fragmented, wide-ranging, and multidimensional. Historically, the concept of tourism was first developed in the period between the two world wars.

Tourism was defined as a sum of relations and phenomena resulting from the travel and stay of nonresidents, in so far as [travel] does not lead to permanent residence and is not connected with any permanent or temporary earning activity. Since 1942, the concept of tourism has been broadened by including various forms of business and pleasure travel.

McIntosh, Goeldner, and Ritchie defined tourism as a short-term movement of people to places other than their normal place of residence and work, including the activities of persons travelling to and staying in locations outside their places of residence and work for not more than twelve months, for the purpose of:

(1) leisure (recreation, vacation, health, study, religion, and sport); and

(2) business, family, mission, and meetings.

Several characteristics of tourism may be identified based on the analyzed definitions:

1. Two main elements:

   (a) movement, which refers to the journey (travel) to and from a destination (the dynamic element of tourism); and

   (b) the overnight stay outside the permanent residence in various destinations (the static element of tourism)

2. Movement to and from the destination is temporary (temporary change of residence), short-term, with intention to return

3. Destinations are visited for purposes other than taking up permanent residence or employment

4. The activities tourists engage in during their journey, and the stay outside the normal place of residence and work, are distinct from those of the local residents and working populations of the places visited The review of various definitions also illustrates a number of conceptual problems in defining tourism. There is no agreement on how far an individual has to travel, how many nights the individual has to stay away from home, or what activities must be engaged in, etc. There are also cross-national differences in defining the concept of tourism.

Four groups of participants are involved and are influenced by tourism:

(1) tourists,

(2) businesses providing goods and services that the tourist market demands,

(3) the government of the host community, and

(4) the host community.

McIntosh, Goeldner, and Ritchie defined tourism as the sum of the phenomena and relationships arising from the interaction of these four groups in the process of attracting and hosting tourists and other visitors. These groups cooperate to accomplish a set of goals at the micro and macro levels within constantly changing legal, political, economic, social, and technological environments.

Characteristics of Tourism

Tourism is very dynamic. It is generally agreed that tourism is fragmented. It is made up of various sectors or subindustries such as transportation, accommodation, attractions, amenities, catering, entertainment, eating and drinking establishments, shops, activity facilities (leisure and recreation), and many others. These sectors provide products and services for individuals or groups of tourists who travel away from home.

Consequently, tourism is an amalgam of the products and services that its various subsectors make available for tourists. The provision of these products and services depends on the linkages between various sectors and their mutual interactions. Tourism is the most wide-ranging industry, in the sense that it demands products from many sectors of the economy and employs millions of people in different sectors.

For example, airplanes and buses must be manufactured to transport tourists; computers must be produced to make hotel booking and airline reservations;

steel, concrete, and glass are needed to build hotels and restaurants; fabrics are needed to make clothes; meat, wheat, and vegetables must be grown to feed visitors. No other industry has so many linkages and interactions with so many sectors of the economy, and delivers so many different kinds of products and services to its consumers.

Tourism is multidimensional. McIntosh, Goeldner, and Ritchie noted that tourism embraces virtually all aspects of human life and society. Tourism is a major economic activity of the travel, lodging, retail, entertainment subsector, and many other subsectors that supply tourist needs. It is a major sociocultural activity that provides different tourist markets with cultural experiences.

Tourism involves production, marketing, and consumption of numerous products such as car rentals, hotel rooms, meals, etc. It requires researching, planning, managing, and controlling tourist enterprises. It is about the location of tourist areas, their physical planning, and changes that tourism development brings to the landscape and community.

The industry depends on various intermediaries and organizations that perform tourism activities. Tourism also involves a historical analysis of tourism activities and various institutions. It is difficult to apply the concept of an industry to tourism in view of the special nature and complexity of the potential contributors to the tourism product.

Tourism is about activities and services. It is about the buying, selling, managing, and marketing of numerous activities and services, which range from renting hotel rooms, selling souvenirs, and managing an airline, to marketing special events. However, since these activities and services represent the supply in the market (tourists constitute the demand) and are part of the economy, they might be described as the tourism "industry".

There is a strong link between tourism and travel. Travel refers to the spatial displacement of people and the activities of people taking trips to places outside their residence for any purpose except daily commuting to and from work. Travel may be undertaken for tourism purposes, or other purposes such as migration, commuting, or exploring. It includes both business and convention tourism as distinguished from "pure" pleasure tourism. Thus, travel has wider meaning and application than tourism.

Hospitality is concerned with the provision of accommodation and catering services for guests. It also refers to the reception and entertainment of travellers, the way they are treated by industry employees (with empathy, kindness, and friendliness), and an overall concern for the traveller's well-being and satisfaction.

Tourists are not the only consumers of hospitality services; local residents also use them. Leisure is considered to be part of free time available to the individual after necessary work and duties are accomplished, to be spent at the discretion of the individual. It refers to the time free from obligations, filled with specific activities, without pressure of necessity.

The problem is, however, in distinguishing between work and leisure activities, and activities undertaken for the purpose of subsistence (e.g., eating). The same activities can be regarded as leisure and as obligations by different individuals. For instance, gardening can be regarded as a leisure activity by some people and as work by others.

Eating, shopping, social activities, and even sleeping may be considered as leisure rather than necessity. The difficulties in categorizing leisure activities were illustrated by Cosgrove and Jackson in Mieczkowski. Consequently, what is viewed as leisure or work depends upon personality, traditions, and/or education of an individual or, as Shaw and Williams noted, upon the individual's attitude of mind, feelings, perceptions, or social position.

Tourism activity is only possible during time available for leisure. However, much of leisure time is spent at home or close to the place of residence; therefore, it is beyond the scope of tourism. Tourism can also be substituted for leisure (e.g., swimming while on vacation can be substituted for swimming in the local sport and recreation centre).

Moreover, vacation experiences may affect the expectations of leisure experiences at home. For example, experiences of playing golf can create the expectation that golf courses should be provided in every local recreation and leisure centre. Experiencing high-quality facilities in local recreation centres may create high expectations for vacation resorts.

Often, leisure is used synonymously with recreation. Recreation refers to the experiences and activities (or inactivities) undertaken during leisure time to recreate physically, psychologically, spiritually, and mentally after work in order to prepare the individual for future work. Recreation activities may include play, games, sports, cultural functions, informal education, sightseeing, entertainment, relaxation, and amusements, as well as travel and tourism.

Clawson and Knetsch in Mieczkowski argued that recreation is the attitude toward activities. An activity is recreation when it involves no feeling of obligation. Recreation is only possible during leisure time. However, not all leisure can be regarded as recreation (e.g., studying, visiting parents). The same activities may be regarded as recreation by one individual yet work by another.

The assessment of what activities are recreational depends on the individual's attitudes and feelings. For example, sport activities can be viewed as recreation, or as a job in professional sports. Tourism is a form of recreation. Recreational tourism is the most significant part of tourism. However, tourism includes elements such as business tourism, which cannot be classified as recreation.

Recreation also involves elements such as urban recreation, which cannot be classified as tourism. Further, tourism can occur within work time (business tourism) whereas recreation occurs during leisure time. Some forms of tourism, such as health tourism, pilgrimages, and visiting friends and relatives are often not associated with recreation.

Also, tourism is always associated with temporary change of residence and overnight stay outside the permanent residence. In contrast, most recreation occurs at home within the local community. In addition, the purchase of recreation equipment often requires financial expenditures that otherwise could have been allocated to tourism and travel. Also, tourism has far more significant commercial implications for the economy than recreation, which is often provided for, free of charge, by the government or social organizations.

Further, tourism does not require learning special skills, as opposed to recreation, which may require the acquisition of special skills such as sport skills. In short, the concepts of tourism, hospitality, and leisure are different, although they are related. Tourism and hospitality are concerned with the provision of goods and services; leisure is a concept of time; and recreation is a concept of activity. Much tourism takes place during leisure time. Recreation is often the main purpose for participation in tourism. All these concepts are characterized by very complex relationships in the creation and delivery of their services to tourists.

The Manila Declaration on World Tourism

The Manila Declaration on World Tourism was agreed in 1980 at the World Tourism Conference, convened by the World Tourism Organization (WTO) with the participation of 107 delegations of States and 91 delegations of observers.

The Declaration touches upon all aspects and roles of Tourism and considers the responsibility of States for the development and enhancement of tourism in present-day societies as more than a purely economic activity of nations and peoples.

The Declaration acknowledges Tourism as an activity which is essential to the life of the Nations and recognises the right to annual paid holidays.

The Declaration continues by saying that Tourism is a very important factor in national economies, that domestic as well as tourism from abroad should be expanded and that it represents a great source of employment, as well as a source of mutual knowledge and understanding. Youth tourism should also be encouraged.

Most importantly, point 18 of the Agreement recognises that "The satisfaction of tourism requirements must not be prejudicial to the social and economic interest of the population in tourist areas, to the environment or, above all, to natural resources which are the fundamental attraction of tourism, and historical and cultural sites".

In the practice of tourism, spiritual elements must take precedence over technical and material elements. Governments should mobilise the means of education and information at their disposal; preparation for tourists, travellers and holiday could usefully form part of the process of youth education and training.

Recreation and Tourism: Recent Trends

Tourism has been the fastest-growing component of world economy for the past decade. Continuing growth in recreation and tourism is likely, although in the near future, the rate of growth may be slower than was the case in the early 1990s. Recreation and tourism is not just fun: it is both big business and an often-cited component of individual well-being. In terms of economic importance, travel and tourism is estimated to account for more than 10 percent of world economic activity; in the United States, travel and tourism is estimated to account for more than 12 percent of gross domestic product, and more than 13 percent of employment.

Although the importance of recreation and tourism is widely acknowledged, estimates of its scale and relative importance continue to be debated largely because recreation and tourism are not conventional economic sectors with routinely-reported statistics .

The growth of recreation and tourism as an economic activity may present opportunities for some communities to adjust to reductions in production and employment in timber and other commodity sectors. In some cases, recreation and tourism has long been an under-recognized component of the natural resource-related economy. The difficulty of establishing precise definitions and the absence of consistent, explicit data on recreation and tourism as an economic sector complicates any effort to understand the economic dimensions and economic dynamics of these activities.

Although the recreation activity of residents does not, by itself, bring additional income into local economies, recreation opportunities and environmental amenities are often significant factors in determining migration (including the selection of retirement and second homes) and tourism. Consequently, resource management for amenity and recreation services is likely to affect the both the size and structure of the local economy. Equally important, tourism (recreation by non-residents) is often an export sector for local and regional economies. That is, tourism is part of the economic activities that provide new employment and income on which the secondary component of the local economy depends. However, there are divergent views on what constitutes the base of an economy. Leaving definitions aside, there is also uncertainty (and dispute) over the effects of land management activities on local economic structure.

What is important is that the net economic benefits of tourism, such as job creation, are comparable in principle to traditional economic base industries. There are obvious and possibly significant differences (as compared to commodity-based industries) in, among other things, wages paid and skills required. But part of the growing awareness of changing social and economic conditions is an acknowledgement of how economies have broadened and the need to understand the dynamic determinants of change.

Some communities facing declining comparative advantage in commodity production may have (or be able to develop) comparative advantage in supplying the services associated with recreation and tourism. Foreseeable changes in demographics, technology, and broad-scale economic conditions make it possible to imagine sustaining or even substantially increasing the contribution of recreation and tourism to state and local economies in the west.

Although the economic opportunities associated with recreation and tourism are important, especially for some rural communities, these opportunities vary widely. In addition, the scale and distribution of the economic benefits of this sector are not well understood. In the short term, any source of economic growth is typically welcome. However, over the longer term, increasing dependence on recreation and tourism may simply replace the cycles and impacts of commodity production and extraction-based industries with a different set of challenges, both for communities and for forest management and policy.

The increasing importance of recreation and tourism to communities especially tourism presents a set of social challenges that accompany the economic opportunities. Changes in the structure of local economies, and greater dependence on the provision of services (often in place of employment in extractive industries and manufacturing) contribute to fundamental changes in social conditions at the community scale. Some of these changes are the consequences of broad-scale trends; some of these changes are closely related to specific natural resource management policies and management decisions.

As compared to commodity goals for forest management, recreation and tourism may present greater challenges for collaborative decision-making and management. Whereas sustained commodity production is assumed to be synonymous with community stability, sustained policy and management support for recreation and tourism may contribute to profound and unwelcome changes in communities. For example, an emphasis on providing recreation services from forests may satisfy local goals for amenities and services, but increasing tourism (non-resident recreation) may lead to conflicts or reductions in the quantity or quality of services for residents.

Recreation and tourism development presents multiple pathways for most communities, and in few cases will these paths provide equivalent or identically distributed benefits. The policy and management challenges for federal resource management agencies are at least as complex as those associated with management for commodity production. Consideration and comparison of local, regional, and national interests, in the context of broad-scale policy objectives as well as national and international trends is required, but the metric for doing this remains unclear.

It is difficult to describe and quantify how individual perceptions of well-being are affected by the quantity and mix of opportunities for leisure activities and the trade-off with opportunities for other types of economic development. We do know that environmental aesthetics and opportunities to appreciate them are important components of well-being, and that there is a wide range of preferences associated with management for aesthetics.

Environmental aesthetics include scenery and associated opportunities to recreate in natural resource based settings. There is considerable evidence, including survey data, to suggest that quality of life issues are taken quite seriously by many residents of Alaska. Therefore, forest management is further challenged to satisfy complex, often intangible, but nevertheless critically-important social objectives.

Increasing recognition of the economic and social importance of recreation and tourism must be accompanied by recognition of the need to formulate and evaluate public policies affecting this sector and its prospective future development. National Forests have long been recognized for their role in providing opportunities for a variety of outdoor recreation activities. In the country as a whole, and especially in the west, National Forests are a dominant provider of a variety of nature-based, dispersed recreation services.

Present and future forest policies affecting types, locations, and levels of recreation use are likely to have effects on human communities as well as on forest ecosystems that are at least as profound as the effects of decisions regarding commodity programs. In order to be effective, forest planning should consider recreation and tourism both as an economic sector and as a social activity. In both the short term and over the long term, forest policies and management have affected the timing and direction of many of the economic adjustments associated with recreation and tourism. Some of the effects of forest policy and management have been intended, and some have been unintended; the consequences of policy and management have not been uniformly positive. Documenting this activity and its relation to natural resource conditions and management is increasingly important for sound public policy making.

As at present, the future will provide a variety business opportunities, and there is likely to continue to be variety in scale and type of operations; although competition is likely to increase, interdependence and cooperation may also increase. Information technology in advertising and marketing for businesses, and technology in equipment will play an increasingly important role for both businesses and individuals. The transportation system and policies regarding access will be key considerations that will shape the future, in terms of both scale and type of activities.

There is potential for, perhaps even the likelihood of increasing conflict among recreation users seeking widely divergent experiences; the likelihood will be reduced but not eliminated by increasing the capacity of the recreation infrastructure.

Among the developments they highlight are a degree of uniformity in the bundle of services packaged for tourists (tourism is becoming a commodity, with accompanying cost and price-based competition); and a counter-trend toward niche marketing for places and firms. Economies of large scale and a variety of developments in transportation enable the former; developments in information technology enable the latter.

Much of the concern about contemporary land management planning can be characterized as the need to better understand the extent to which it is possible to simultaneously achieve economic, social, and natural resource policy objectives. In the past decade, increasing attention has been given to the need to emphasize protection and restoration of ecosystem services in place of commodities; there is also greater emphasis being given to other natural resource-based services, such as recreation. In many places, increasing recreation and tourism development is almost inevitable given prospective economic changes (both structural change and income growth) and demographic changes. This leads to two fundamental questions. First, is the growth of recreation and tourism likely to contribute to sustainable community development? Second, what are the tradeoffs between recreation use and the biophysical conditions of an ecosystem?

Recreation and tourism is a significant economic sector and a component of the quality of life. Therefore, resource allocation decisions affecting the 'physical plant' of recreation and tourism will be important. The physical plant must be seen to include the infrastructure (campgrounds, cabins, roads, trails, etc.) and the landscape in which it exists. Increasingly, management and policy choices will reflect trade-offs between accommodating (or even promoting) recreation and tourism and other objectives of forest management, as well as trade-offs among types of recreation and tourism activity. Understanding both the reality and dimensions of these possible tradeoffs are future research questions.

There appear to be divergent trends between recreation (resident) and tourism (visitor) activities. Economic and demographic factors will contribute to increases in the relative importance of tourism (visitor activity) within the recreation and tourism mix.

In general, trends in recreation and tourism use and demand appear to have slowed across a number of activities in the late 1990s as compared to rapid growth in the early part of the decade. Various measures of recreation and tourism use support this conclusion, but the data are insufficient to draw long-term implications from this observation. Among the possible explanations for slowing of the rates of increase in tourism are: local and national economic and demographic trends, cycles and competition in the tourism industry and capacity constraints in some activities or key infrastructure. Capacity constraints include both physical limitations and psychic limitations based on perceptions of the quality of acceptability of experiences.

Concepts of carrying capacity for recreation activities are not well understood; therefore, managing for maximum numbers of users is likely to require greater attention to quality issues.

Continuing growth in recreation and tourism is likely, although in the near future, rates of growth may be slower than was the case in the early 1990s. In the future, recreation and tourism activities are, on average, likely to be shorter in duration and more intense, in keeping with broader social and economic trends. This is likely to lead to increased opportunities for commercially-mediated activities. At the same time, continuing evolution and competition in the commercial recreation and tourism sector will, itself, contribute to innovation and efforts to exploreand createmarket opportunities. The result is likely to be continued increases in demand for management decisions that support commercial activities. Competition within the commercial sector, and competition between commercial users and the general public will continue and increase.

2

Cultural Tourism

Tourism that focuses upon the rich past of people or areas as preserved and portrayed in monuments, historic sites, architecture and artefacts is commonly callled as cultural tourism. However these definitions only include part of cultural tourism, since culture cannot simply be limited to the past. Culture is also a dynamic and living phenomenon. Moreover such definitions focus on the demand approach. To identify cultural tourism, both demand and supply must be taken into account. Thus cultural tourism encompasses all cultural activities undertaken by visitors and the supply of products for cultural visitors during their visit.

The cultural "activity", which may consist of attending artistic or other events as a spectator or non-professional participant, visiting museums, exhibitions, etc., can be combined with other activities; nevertheless, the visit can be considered as part of "cultural tourism". Cultural activities may be undertaken with any main purpose of the visit, since any purpose of travel away from the usual environment can generate cultural tourism.

Cultural tourism can be evaluated by combining information on :

— tourism activities undertaken during trips

— consumption of tourism products

— the destination

For household demand-side surveys the statistical reporting unit can be the household and the individual within the household. For surveys held in the very location where the visitor carries on his cultural activity, the statistical unit is the visitor or travelling party. As far as the supply of cultural tourism is concerned, the statistical units to be considered are found at the enterprise level, the local unit level and the Kind of Activity unit level.

Cultural tourism is not limited to cultural towns and cities in urban areas, so that the cultural tourism destination or location of cultural activities should also be identified at local level. Most activities relating to culture fall within recreational, cultural and sporting activities. However, attending language courses, exhibitions, cultural meetings and partaking in guided tours can also be considered as part of cultural tourism, and are included in the list below. The link between cultural supply in an area and its effects on other tourism-related activities (suppliers) exists. For example, the cultural supply, or more specifically the use made of this supply (consumption) will affect the supply of other tourism activities. Likewise, there are two types of cultural tourism product :

— typically cultural products ;

— general products part of whose consumption is linked to the consumption of cultural products.

Thus, total cultural tourism supply comprises typical cultural activities (products) and the supply of other tourism-related activities (products) when the consumption of the latter is linked to the consumption of cultural products. Information on the propensity to travel will provide estimates on the volume of tourism and, within this, the share of cultural tourism can be estimated. More detailed questions on the propensity to engage in cultural tourism may also be asked. To obtain a good picture of cultural visits, all the variables concerning the characteristics of the trip should be taken into account. The determining variable is activities undertaken during the visit. This will be linked to all the other variables.

Linking detailed information on the destination(s), (making the distinction between intermediary, main and final destination) and on destination types can be used to assess the cultural component within a visit. Likewise, the duration of the visit, particularly the distinction between overnights visits and same-day visits, will provide information on the degree of the cultural element within a visit. The period of year chosen can in some cases be directly linked to the cultural activity Questions on the travel party composition and organisation of the visit could perhaps be made more detailed in order to distinguish certain elements e.g. school trips, package tours specialising in cultural tours. Finally, if possible, one can try to single out tourism expenditure on cultural activities.

The variables to be taken into account are:

Supply:

— Number of establishments, local units

— Number of festivals, parks, exhibitions

— Number of opening days (seasonality)

— Period of access

Capacity:

— Maximal reception capacity, e.g. number of seats

Use of supply

— Number of arrivals, of visitors

— Number of tickets issued (to groups, with reduction, free of charge, etc.)

— Number of units sold (tickets)

— Entrance fees

Economic variables:

— Investments value, incl. value of restorations

— employment: number of full-timers, number of part-timers incl. guides

— Turnover

— Promotion evaluation: publicity costs, number of commercials in media, number of posters distributed, agreements with tour-operators

— Inventory of promoted products: specific products (i.e. tours, events, exhibitions, etc.)

Statistics on culture can give an overall view of cultural consumption for different sectors which, with a few exceptions, are more or less connected to tourism also. However, in statistics on culture it is very often impossible to separate the share of local people from the share of visitors, but quite often estimates are available or can be derived from other sources such as tourist accommodation statistics or passenger transport statistics.

Time use surveys can offer important information about the time spent by residents on different cultural activities during trips. However, because of the sample size of such surveys, information can only be at country and not regional level. Household surveys and sample surveys at international arrival and departure points may provide limited information on the cultural activities undertaken by visitors; however this would require a detailed questionnaire and thus a large sample size. Better and more detailed information can be collected by conducting sample surveys at cultural destinations. Demand-side sample surveys at the destination or cultural sites of visitors attracted by the cultural supply can be carried out in parallel to investigations of holiday makers in order to estimate the share of the cultural tourism market. Supply-side surveys on enterprises or local units classified according to cultural tourism supply criteria using a representative sample can provide more detailed information on capacity, use of supply and economic data.

Effects of Tourism on Culture

Tourism today is a major economic and social phenomenon. It is one of the three main international commercial exchange sectors along with petrol and motorized vehicles. Integrated in the leisure world, it has become a mass phenomenon, and at the same time a social necessity. In 1991, about 450 million tourists travelled abroad and ten times more tourists circulated within their own country; there were 18 times more tourist arrivals than 40 years before, with an annual increase average of 7.3%. The region which holds the highest increase in the 1980's is Southeast Asia, South Asia and the Pacific.

Cultural Tourism: Experience of Cambodia

Most of the income from tourism in these countries originates from industrialized countries. This trend represents a strong hope for tourism in Cambodia. Alongside agriculture and industry, the government has accorded tourism priority status for development, Since the Paris Agreement of October 1991, the number of tourists in Cambodia has steadily increased. An estimated 87,720 visitors came in 1992. To meet the increasing demand, many hotels and restaurants have been built.

At least 40 travel agencies are active in Phnom Penh, with offices also in Siem Reap, where Angkor, Cambodia's main tourist attraction, is located. Air travel, both domestic and international, is on the rise. Cambodia houses a treasure other countries of the region do not have. This historic site of Angkor is one of the wonders of the world. It was inscribed on the UNESCO World Heritage List in December 1992.

Cambodia is also home to numerous other historic sites, beautiful beaches and splendid landscapes which are unknown to many because the country has been isolated from the outside world for many years. The arrival of tourists will bring necessary hard currency into the country and help solve employment problems. However, it will also inevitably bring changes in the traditional social organization and modify the natural environment.

The influence of tourism on the environment has led many countries to realize the necessity to take into consideration less tangible factors to assess the effects of tourism development. They include the impact on the social structure, intersectoral imbalance, and disruption in the ways of living. Cambodia must not sacrifice short term benefits for a long term catastrophic impact on the environment. International assistance is needed to establish the country's tourism master plan.

There was a significant number of tourists coming to Cambodia in 1950s. Since then, the amount of visitors increased steadily from 21,180 in 1%3 to 46,706 in 1969. The majority of visitors come from the United States, Japan and France, followed by other European countries, Australia and neighbouring countries in the region, especially Thailand. The subject of tourism also encompasses the subject of land and infrastructure management.

This has been one of the major concerns of the authorities, therefore several studies were made. Prior to the disturbances of the 1970s and 198Os, regional tourist destinations were developed in Kirirom, Sihanoukville, Bokor and Battambang. With the assistance of UNESCO, a new tourist area was envisaged on the Phnom Kulen, while the ancient Khmer road was to be restructured to reach several temples in the jungle located between Angkor and Sambor Prei Kuk, such as Beng Mealea, Koh Ker and Preah Khan.

A new urban development centre was also to be created 4 km away from Angkor Wat, next to the old city of Siem Reap, in order to accommodate a group of hotels, commercial and sports facilities, as well as recreational activities. Since the mid-1970, no records concerning tourism have been kept. The destruction of human and natural resources starting from 1979 onwards did not allow the revival of tourism until the end of the 1980s.

The former General Direction of Tourism, created in August 1988, has recently become the Ministry of Tourism. Its main roles are to ensure integrated tourism development in Cambodia and to promote tourist activities inside and outside the country. To assist local authorities, regional, provincial and municipal tourism offices are being created. They depend technically and financially on the Ministry of Tourism. The main provincial and municipal offices are:

— Phnom Perth Tourism, created in 1983

— Angkor Tourism, created in 1986

— Kompong Som/Sihanoukville Tourism

— Kep Tourism

— Eleven other tourism offices exist in the provinces, but have little activity

In 1968, Cambodia had 16.000 km of roads and highways. Approximately 40% of all roads and bridges were destroyed by over 20 years of war. Even though foreign aid was slow to come, the Royal Cambodian Government managed to repair those tourism infrastructures vital to Cambodia's national reconstruction. By the end of 1995. Highway 4 linking Phnom Penh to Kompong Som, and Veal Rinh to Kompong Som is expected to be completed.

Waterways have not yet been professionally used for tourist purposes. The Ministry of Tourism has suggested cruise lines on the Mekong River and the Tonle Sap Lake.

Some investors have expressed their interest in the project of Railways are only used to carry merchandise and local passengers.

Most tourists arrive by air. During the 1980's, the only planes came from Viet Nam. Laos and the Soviet Union. Gradually, other companies have set up regular flights to Phnom Penh. notably from Thailand. Presently, there are several weekly or daily flights from Bangkok, Kuala Lumpur, Vientiane, Ho Chi Mirth City, Moscow, Singapore, Taipei and Hong Kong. In 1991, 81% of all tourists entered Cambodia by air.

Domestic flights have also increased and new provincial airports have reopened in Siem Reap, Battambang, Sihanoukville, Koh Kong, Rattanakiri, and Kompong Cham. Until 1991, communications inside and outside Cambodia were extremely difficult. They have improved considerably with the establishment of two satellite links, one from the former Soviet Union and the other from Australia.

The Thai company Samart has introduced the use of mobile phones. Most of the hotels and restaurants are now equipped with telephone and fax services. The number of hotels has sharply increased, especially since 1991 with the influx of the UN forces. At the time of writing in Phnom Penh there were 129 hotels with a total of 5,024 rooms.

In Siem Reap, there were 8 hotels with 315 rooms in addition to several guest houses. There are many restaurants serving foreign and local specialties. However, the service needs to be improved in order to meet international standards. Cambodia possesses many tourist attractions throughout the country. They are notably the following:

— Natural resources

— The Mekong River, the Tonle Sap Lake, numerous waterfalls;

— Seaside, beaches, islands;

— Scenic forests and mountains;

— Paddy fields and other landscapes of natural beauty.

— Cultural heritage

— Ancient temples numbering more than 1,070. mostly built between the 9th and 13th centuries;

— Old pagodas, shrines, monasteries, and mosques;

— Palaces and museums;

— Ethnic minority settlements.

There are three official border entries: Bavet, on the border with Viet Nam; Kompong Som/Sihanoukville on the seaside in the South; and Phnom Penh via the international airport. At Poipet, in the West of the country, Thais can enter but cannot go further than the Poipet market. Entry formalities are facilitated as visas can be obtained directly at the Ministry of Foreign Affairs or in the various Cambodian consulates in foreign countries.

The immigration service at the international airport can deliver visas upon entry for a short period, for a cost of 20 US$. The Royal Cambodian Government allows tourists to enter Cambodia without visas for a period of seven days. Up to the end of 1992, 122 travel agencies were registered. They are mainly receiving agencies for tourists sent by agencies in foreign countries, such as Japan, Thailand, France, Italy, Taiwan, Hong Kong, and the United States.

Most owners of these agencies are foreigners. The agencies do not only take care of foreign visitors but also of Cambodians wishing to travel abroad. A tourism office in the capital was created in 1983. and three years later, an agreement was signed with the Tourism Agency of Viet Nam. Until 1991, Phnom Penh Tourism was in charge of three hotels: the Monorom, the Cambodiana Inn, and the Cambodiana Hotel. These hotels have now been privatized as joint-ventures.

The tourist activities in those two seaside areas have risen since 1991, with mainly an increase in local tourists. In order to efficiently manage the international tourists, and show them the best of Cambodia, as well as to preserve the prestige of the capital, all tourists must go through Phnom Penh. Tours of one to twelve days are proposed with one to eight days in Siem Reap, the site of the Angkor World Heritage Site.

In addition to Siem Reap, several tourist sites exist around Phnom Penh and further away to the seaside. The diversity of the activities has increased since 1992. With the introduction of the market economy and the signature of the Paris Agreement, the country is again open to the international community. The global exposure and increasing arrivals of tourists have a decisive impact on the national economy.

National and international investment in the tourism industry goes mainly towards the building or renovation of hotels and restaurants. Investment will be expanded not only in terms of infrastructure but also in terms of improvement of human resources. In 1992, there were great efforts made to promote Cambodian tourism, through the travel agencies, international organizations and the media.

Several groups from abroad visited Cambodia, and Cambodian representatives in turn attended international seminars on tourism organized by the World Tourism Organization (WTO) in Bali and in Spain, and PATA in Hong Kong 8.and in Japan, as well as other meetings. The Ministry of Tourism of the Royal Cambodian Government plans to celebrate Cambodia Tourism Year in 1996.

Tourism development must be well planned and controlled with strong management structures. The unforeseen boom development of tourism in 1992 disrupted the lives of the population, isolated from the rest of the world for so many years. Its long-term impact on the culture and the environment have not yet been studied thoroughly. The Ministry of Tourism will be co-operating with many ministries and organizations recently created - such as the Secretariat of State for Environment and the National Committee for the Management of the Territory - in order to avoid any possible misunderstanding.

As the revival of tourism is a new phenomenon in Cambodia, its effects on culture and environment have yet to be taken into consideration. However, the changes which occurred in 1992 pose problems for the responsible authorities, concerned for the long-term development of the country. The question of the protection of the environment is a new concept in Cambodia.

The Secretariat of State for Environment has just been created, and already it has several issues to address. Similarly, the Ministry of Culture faces difficulties in the preservation and restoration of the cultural heritage. The National Committee for the Management of the Territory is organized out of a need to resolve differences between the regions.

The national two-year Tourism Plan for 1994-1995 considers tourism not only as a source for foreign currency and employment but also as a contributor to the protection and the conservation of the culture and traditions of the country. Cambodia is now experiencing a historic turn, notably in terms of its economy. It offers great potential for tourism-related investments. At the same time, it faces the challenges of protecting its national heritage and the environment as a whole.

Since Cambodia has been isolated from the rest of the world for two decades, it is only natural for foreigners to be curious about the country and its culture. Visitors are especially eager to see the splendour of Angkor and the exotic landscapes. Besides the 20,000 UN personnel coming into the country, the year 1992 saw the arrival of foreign businessmen, officials, journalists and tourists.

Accommodation, hotels and office space were suddenly in great demand and were established in a rather anarchic way, as the time and means were not available to arrange this in an organized mmer. In the development of hotels, guest houses and restaurants, no consideration was given to the maintenance of public order or to the traditional way of living of the local population.

The rapid increase of city dwellers, comprising also foreigners and locals coming from the provinces, has seriously disturbed the capital city of Phnom Penh. Neither urban zoning nor regulations on architecture has been elaborated, creating more problems for traffic and parking facilities. To date the location of new hotels and buildings is arbitrary and does not account for the ancient urbanism of Phnom Penh and of other cities like Battambang and Siem Reap.

Their architecture clashes with the traditional settings, thus damaging the general character of the town. Moreover, the interior decoration of some of those hotels and restaurants do not have a Khmer character. To maintain the consistency of the ancient urban cities of Cambodia, the decor and architecture of these new buildings need to be Khmer. The establishment of hotels has aggravated the problem caused by the absence of sewage treatment throughout the country.

As a consequence, the pollution level of the rivers is increasing, and the country does not have the financial and technical capabilities to solve the problem. The lack of electrical power has forced the installation of diesel generators, which in turn cause noise and air pollution due to petrol fumes.

Unplanned development strategies will have disastrous environmental effects. Since the Paris Agreement, Cambodia has changed from a centralized to a market economy. With the steady increase of foreign investment, the current administrative structures do not have the absorptive and management capacity to deal with the present situation. There is a lack of organization in the distribution of responsibilities and regulations to manage foreign investments and therefore the co-ordination of development projects.

An important aspect of tourism is the creation of jobs. Because of the dearth of experienced personnel in hotel and restaurant sectors, management jobs are often given to foreigners. This problem is frequent within the travel agencies. Appropriate training should be given to young Cambodians willing to work for the tourism sector. The local travel agencies are mainly responsible for receiving tourists, taking them from and to the airport and making bookings.

They do not organize travel and package tours which are usually paid in foreign countries, thereby no local income is generated. Consequently, the national agencies do not have the necessary funds to promote and expand themselves. One of the main social problems caused by the massive arrival of tourists and foreigners is the increasing number of nightclubs and prostitution.

The tourist sites in Cambodia are not yet laid out and organized. For example, the site of Tonle Bati, not far from Phnom Penh, could be a great tourist attraction if it were well managed. Without a thorough and effective plan for tourism development, the disorder will only increase. The choice must not only be left to the foreign investors but should also be decided at the national level.

A French company has established a tourist centre on an island of the Mekong River. Two other Cambodian companies are exploiting large pieces of land not far from Pochentong Airport, forcing farmers there to leave and abandon their traditional activities. The project to extend the capital towards the west and the one to improve the capacity of Pochentong Airport have considerably augmented the price of land.

On the seaside, the influx of local tourists has already spoiled the beauty of the coastline by polluting it. Exposure to new ideas has also modified the people's lifestyle. The management of the coastal areas needs appropriate studies and specific regulations to prevent further deterioration of the environment, social and cultural values. The effects of tourism on culture and environment in Cambodia are not yet as dramatic as in other countries of the region.

This is the reason why the tourism industry should be well planned and its development carefully controlled in order to create sustainable tourism, integrated within the cultural and environmental context of the country. Sustainable tourism was defined by the Globe 90 Conferences on Environment and Industry as ((... the management of tourism resources in such a way that fulfills economic, social and aesthetic needs while maintaining cultural integrity, essential ecological process, biological diversity and life support systems. "

In other words, it is necessary to preserve the environmental resources and the cultural integrity, while bringing the socio-economic benefit of tourism to the people living in the country. In this context, Cambodia has requested international assistance to elaborate a master plan for tourism development. UNDP and WTO have already drafted a report called "Tourism Sector Review, Cambodia".

In any event, all these plans are only the starting point because of the lack of funds and of experience in this field. If well managed, most of the natural and cultural resources of the country can bring numerous benefits to the tourism industry, developed only on the basis of the maintenance of the environmental and cultural quality of the country. This objective cannot be obtained without the participation of the other ministries and institutions concerned.

The final result will also depend on the full participation of the local population. In order to co-ordinate the act·on of those various ministries and private organizations. the establishment of an intersectoral body would be an asset.

The war left unexperienced personnel in the tourism administration and industry. Therefore, the most urgent task is to train competent staff for the public as well as the private sectors. The second priority is to inform the public, establish properly managed tourist parks and infrastructure and prevent or mitigate the negative effects of tourism development on the population, the cultural heritage and the environment of the country.

Access to the main tourist centres is one of the major obstacles to development. This task is under the responsibility of the Ministry of Transport. Depending on the availability of funds, the Ministry's main objective is to renovate most of the roads. The airport facilities have considerably improved and the airports should soon be upgraded.

Until now, Cambodia has had no structure for the protection and conservation of the environment. WWF has proposed to UNDP a project for the management of the environment through the establishment of a group of environmental advisers, called "Cambodian Environmental Advisory Team" (CEAT) to work with the national authorities.

In Combodia, the archaeological complex of Angkor is the most exceptional site of the region, and it could receive a minimum of 2,000 tourists a day. The site was inscribed on the UNESCO World Heritage List in December 1992 on the condition that the Cambodian authorities:

i) promulgate adequate protective legislation;

ii) establish a national protection agency;

iii) delimit permanent boundaries and buffer zones; and

iv) establish international monitoring and co-ordination.

In response, Cambodia has requested UNESCO to undertake a large-scale study in order to establish the zoning and an environmental management plan (ZEMP). It involved the interpretation of newly flown large-scale aerial photographs from the Land Use Mapping Office (Ministry of Agriculture) and ground survey to verify results. Reports were prepared on archaeology, hydrology, ecology and wildlife, social conditions, urban development, rural development, tourism development, studies of the legal and and environment regulatory framework, organization and management of protected areas/parks and the protection of archaeological sites and monuments and their presentation to visitors.

Angkor is the main tourist attraction of the country. Beside the development of the archaeological complex, which is the highest priority, other areas in Cambodia need to be improved for tourism: the sites around Phnom Penh, the coastal areas such as Sihanoukville and Kep as well as provinces such as Takeo, Kompong Cham, Battambang, and Rattanakiri.

International assistance is needed not only for the maintenance of peace but also for both material and spiritual reconstruction and development of the country in order to help Cambodia preserve its identity in the international community.

Cambodia is currently in a significant period of transition from isolation toward full-fledged participation in the booming markets of Asia. Peace and technological progress in transport and telecommunications will bring rapid growth in the development of tourism to Cambodia. There are, however, anxieties about the role of tourism and its possible negative effects as development takes place.

The conflict may involve choosing between short and long-term interests as well as commercial exploitation and maintenance of socio-cultural and environmental quality. The cross cultural interaction of various conflicting value systems is another unavoidable consequence of international tourism which may become a matter for concern. Most foreigners equate the Angkor complex, especially Angkor Wat, with Cambodia.

The monuments give the country an instantly recognizable and prestigious profile. The Angkor Cultural Area of the province of Siem Reap, within which the Angkor World Heritage Site is located, covers approximately 5,000 sq. km. The area, spreading over the Angkor plain between the Kulen plateau to the north and the Tonle Sap to the south, encompasses over 1,000 archaeological sites and the remains of at least seven cities built by Khmer kings between the 9th and the 13th centuries.

Current political stability has led to a more peaceful reconstruction period for Cambodia which, in turn, will provide opportunities to revitalize international efforts focused on preserving Angkor. While these efforts have helped to rekindle global awareness and concern for Angkor, a new set of challenges lies ahead for Cambodia. These include how to manage and balance tourism interests, archaeological research opportunities and restoration work with the socio-economic needs of the Cambodian people. This could be implemented through the development of ecologically sustainable agriculture, forestry, aquaculture, water management and tourism in and around the Angkor Cultural Area.

The traditional way of life of the local communities of Siem Reap province can draw considerable cultural and touristic interest. It must therefore be maintained and protected. A tourism development plan should include the conservation of the villagers' traditional village locations and the assistance to revitalize their handicraft techniques for generating supplemental income from the sale of traditional souvenirs to tourists.

Village houses could be restored and renovated so that handicrafts can be presented and sold on location. On the whole, the local people are aware and proud of their heritage and can both contribute to and benefit from a revival of these traditions. The proximity of the town of Siem Reap and the Angkor World Heritage Site provides both an opportunity and a constraint for these conservation efforts.

At the cross-roads involving contradictory but not incompatible interests, Siem Reap can avoid falling victim to incongruous tourism development. It is a small, low density town with an homogeneous traditional architecture. The city's character must be preserved and strict zoning rules must be applied to future development.

Already the Angkor Reserve commands respect from both the developers and the local community. The major issue is how to reconcile conservation and urban development. Despite some agricultural problems, these peasants are deeply attached to their land. Agricultural land for rice cultivation is in short supply. Due to the population increase and political situation, families now have to survive on half a hectare of land where, previously, two were available.

The production of rice is not sufficient to feed the population because of the small size of the freshly cleared ground, the mediocrity of land quality, and the lack of water. Supplementary income is therefore sought through swidden agriculture (slash and burn), the collection of resin from the forest, palm juice for sugar; rattan and jungle vines for the manufacture of fishing baskets and the cutting of firewood to make charcoal.

Technical skills such as silk weaving and handicraft activities which generated complementary income in the past are now largely lost. As these settlements are ancient, populations have over the years developed several kinds of micro-cultures:

— on the river banks: vegetable cultivation;

— on the back of the river banks: dry season rice (srovprang);

— near the hamlets and during the monsoon: floating rice (srov laeng teuk and srov bandaeng teuk);

— near the villages and between the houses: flooded rice (srov vossa) .

Each household owns two hectares of land and has more than enough rice to feed the family. In exchange for the extra rice, they get rattan, resin and jungle vines from surrounding Angkor villages. Moreover, for supplementary income, villagers sell vegetables.

In recognition of the national and global significance of the Angkor monuments as the representation of Khmer civilization, His Majesty Samdech Preah Norodom Sihanouk Varman, in his capacity as Head of State and President of the Supreme National Council of Cambodia, signed the World Heritage Convention in 1991 and presented the Angkor Archaeological Park for inscription on the World Heritage List for the following reasons:

i) it represents a unique artistic achievement, a masterpiece of creative genius;

ii) it has exerted great influence over a span of time, within a cultural area of the world, on developments in architecture, monumental arts and landscaping;

iii) it bears a unique exceptional testimony to a civilization which has disappeared;

iv) it is an outstanding example of an architectural ensemble which illustrates a significant stage in history.

The situation in Cambodia, seen from a tourism point of view, must be evaluated in the context of the political situation and regional development in southeast Asia, particularly in Thailand, Laos and Viet Nam. Having been "closed" to visitors for many years, Cambodia (and therefore Angkor) is now wide open to the international tourism market. Tourists are eager for new experiences and adventures, while tour operators consider Angkor one of the last places to discover and offer a new, previously unexplored destination in their tour programmes and travel catalogues.

Investors, especially in hotel projects, sense this coming boom and see the good earning potential, given the current acute shortage of appropriate lodging facilities in Siem Reap. The pressure to develop tourist facilities and infrastructure will be strong within the next 5-10 years, and the possibility of using the tourist boom to develop the Siem Reap region and the country is high.

However, the problem of controlling and channelling this development is paramount, especially during these key years. The basis of the economy of Siem Reap town and the Angkor area will be tourism.

However, elsewhere modemization of subsistence agriculture and sustainable use of forest and lake resources, capitalized by the profits of tourism, should lead to improvements in living standards for the rural population throughout the whole province.

The Angkor area offers a unique cultural experience. The value of cultural tourism - and here the term is used to define tourism which involves active participation by the culture sector with a view to sharing with visitors the genuine cultural and historical values of the region - lies not simply in its capacity to heighten visitors' pleasure by broadening their knowledge of life in a given tourist destination, it is also important as a means of encouraging sensitivity towards the safeguarding and restoration of cultural assets and of protecting the environment and the population's traditional way of life.

The largest number of tourists came from Japan, followed by France and then by the United States of America, Germany, Italy and Thailand respectively. If the political situation stabilizes, tourism experts anticipate that the annual number of tourists visiting Siem Reap could reach 300,000 plus by the end of the century. Cambodia - with Angkor as its main asset and major tourist attraction - stands to become the most popular tourist destination in Southeast Asia. But first, the needed infrastructure must be built.

Regarding quantitative development of tourism in the Angkor area, the number of tourists visiting the monuments, and the number of hotel rooms in Siem Reap are key considerations for planning. However, the starting point for considering the optimum number of tourists visiting Angkor is the carrying capacity of each individual monument as well as that of the park area as a whole.

This will change over time from the current situation, where there is no effective park organization to meet with tourists' needs and complaints, to the day when a Park Authority will be established in full professional operation, and equipped to cope with thousands of visitors a day.

The limiting factor for the maximum number of tourists who can visit Angkor at any one time is the carrying capacity of the park, not the number of hotel rooms, or the convenience of other aspects of the tourism infrastructure. One of the most obvious dangers for Angkor is development which does not take into account the carrying capacity of the monuments, as the main monuments have a limited capacity to accommodate visitors.

The most visited monuments are Angkor Wat, Bayon, Ta Prohm, Preah Khan, Phnom Bakheng, Baphuon and Banteay Srei. These seven monuments therefore set the limit for the carrying capacity of the archaeological park and determine the number of tourists who can be received there at any one time. Calculating the maximum number of visitors who could visit the monuments is a complex task.

If 3,000 visitors a day is assumed for each of the major sites, with visitors staying between 1 and 2 hours in the monuments, this means that during one day, a maximum of 1,500 persons can go through the temples in the morning and another 1.500 in the afternoon. Based on these considerations and bearing in mind that the distribution of tourists is not equally spread over all months of the year and that there will be a considerable number of domestic tourists and pilgrims added to the estimate above, the maximum capacity of the park might be estimated between 500,000 and 700,000 international tourists per year.

It is also essential that money generated by tourism be reinvested in the proper maintenance of the monuments themselves to maintain the site and protect the temples from the stress caused by visitors. Given the economically impoverished condition of Cambodia, the entrance fee will have to be different for international tourists and local/domestic visitors. While the entrance fee for international visitors should be high and should incorporate a major contribution towards the restoration of the monuments, the entrance fee should be much lower for domestic visitors and should be set according to the income of the average Cambodian.

What is crucial is that the monuments of Angkor should not be reduced to the status of an expendable commercial resource and thus be deprived of the funds needed to secure their proper conservation and to facilitate their presentation to visitors in an appealing and educational way. This would not only damage the cultural heritage of the country, but also destroy the most important resource on which the Cambodian tourism industry is built. An urban development plan is required in order to accommodate the growth anticipated from tourism, in addition to the high rate of population growth and the migration of workers to the area that tourism can be expected to induce. The plan can be financed by the income generated by tourism with an aim to increase the general welfare of the local population as well as to support the growing tourism industry.

An urban plan linked with a transportation plan to move the airport and to modify roads requires the definition of different zones:

— An "urban conservation zone" will maintain the low density residential character which presently exists in central Siem Reap and revitalize the historic character of the old parts of the town. "Urban expansion zonestl would accommodate new urban growth in properly planned locations - residential, commercial and community developments.

— A "tourism development zone" would provide a prime location for planned tourism developments. It could be the location of all major hotel and resort constructions.

An educational and cultural plan has to be integrated with local educational programmes in order to provide for a future generation of hotel managers, guides, labourers, etc. and to integrate the population of Siem Reap into tourism development. Several types of employment are to be expected when the tourism industry develops.

— Direct employment in site restoration and maintenance;

— Employment from expenditure on tourism facilities such as hotels, restaurants, souvenir industry, entertainment, guiding, etc.;

— Indirect employment in businesses affected by tourism such as agriculture, building trades, banks, etc. ;

— Induced employment arising from the money spent by the local residents from their tourism income.

As a rough estimate, between three and four jobs can be calculated per bed or between six and eight jobs per hotel room. In addition to these direct and indirect jobs, the induced employment provided by the effects of tourism income should not be forgotten.

Monuments and artifacts should in turn be presented to visitors in a factual and coherent way, with a view to explaining their historical and cultural significance. This will involve extensive training of guides, the publication of high quality guidebooks and other related educational materials, (e.g. slides and postcards) which may be sold to tourists.

A cultural and educational development plan is also required to ensure that the local population benefits from the tourism industry. At the historic temples of Angkor, outdoor performances could be organized during the dry season. Further opportunities to enhance the presentation of the Khmer cultural heritage could include the concept of son et lumiere, where traditional performing arts are incorporated into a live and vibrant presentation.

Cambodia has a long and rich history of craft-making and was renowned for a number of different crafts, such as silk and cotton textiles weaving, metal work and silversmithery, woodcarving, rattan furniture, bamboo maquettes and basket weaving. This craft-bound tradition is rooted in a period when handicraft articles were created for practical purposes as well as for meeting aesthetic needs, and were thus produced by almost everyone in the society.

In more recent times, there has been a shift in emphasis. While villagers still produce handicraft articles for their own use, for barter or for use in traditional ceremonies, they have started using them primarily as a means of generating additional income for the household, especially in rural areas where arable land is often in short supply.

Traditional craft production should be boosted with a view to enabling more craftsmen to make a living from their work. At the same time, it enhances overall standards of production, which include the revival of the traditional art of silk weaving, silversmithery and ethnic minority handicrafts. Today, it is still possible to revive sericulture. The revival of silk production could provide home-produced thread for a revitalized silkweaving industry taking a full and active role in cultural tourism and providing additional income for rural areas. The market for traditional crafts will increase with the development of cultural tourism.

Like Combodia, Nepal's diversity attracts tourists. Its physical uniqueness offers a wide scope of activities that range from visiting jungle resort camps to trekking in snow-capped mountains. Tourism is important to Nepal as a source of foreign exchange and a major employment generator. At the time of writing the sector accounted for approximately 22 per cent of total foreign earnings.

For a country like Nepal, which lacks abundant resources, the tourism sector is expected to continue to play an important role in the country's development, but not without negative consequences. Rationale of the study Nepal's tourism industry has its share of problems. Although the number of tourists visiting the country has increased every year since 1970, Nepal still receives only a small fraction of the visitors to Southeast Asia, India and Sri Lanka.

Those tourists who do visit, with the exception of trekkers, stay for short durations. The tourism industry is highly capital intensive, with foreign exchange earnings used for importing expendable goods, or used to further promote tourism. Although, the importance of the tourism sector's contributions to the economy cannot be dismissed, this sector generates a host of unfavourable effects on the country's culture and environment.

It has aggravated existing environmental problems and placed more pressure on the fragile economy and national resources. These problems are compounded by an erosion of local customs, an increase in drug abuse and theft of antiques and cultural property. In the existing literature on tourism in Nepal, studies regarding the socio-cultural and environmental impacts of tourism are few.

The studies that have been made are sketchy and isolated; they shed very little light on the subject matter. In order to promote the development of an appropriate kind of tourism that prevents or minimizes cultural and environmental degradation, more in-depth studies are needed for an understanding of the industry's problems.

Cultural tourism: Experience of Nepal

The macro-analysis of tourism is based on the existing data published by the Ministry of Tourism of His Majesty's Government of Nepal and on the current government policy pertaining to tourism. The impact of its tourism activities on the life-style of the That-us population was also analyzed. The other site chosen for the case study is Ghandruk, a village one day travelling distance from Pokhara, the second busiest tourist destination after Kathmandu. Inhabited by the Gurung hill people, it is en-route to the Annapurna Base Camp, where trekkers pass on their route to the Annapurna sanctuary in western Nepal.

Together, they provided an overall picture of the country's various kinds of ongoing tourism activities, thereby showing how these activities have affected the so&o-economic and cultural lives of the Nepalese people. In-depth interviews were held both with the households engaged directly in tourism and also with those who were not.

The uniqueness of Nepal with its panoramic natural beauty and its rich cultural heritage has attracted many people to this country. The number of tourists visiting Nepal is increasing. In 1987, 248.000 tourists visited the country. In 1990 the numbers went up to over 254,000; and, in 1991, there were roughly 293,000 tourists. Although the table shows that the number of tourists visiting Nepal is increasing, there are exceptions.

Among the Europeans, the number of German, Danish, and Italian visitors was highest. At the time of writing, tourist arrivals from India and Japan were increasing. At a slower rate, the percentage of tourists from Australia and the Pacific were also on the rise. The average length of stay of tourists in Nepal, consistent from 1974 to 1990, was around 13 days.

A majority of tourists to Nepal come for pleasure as opposed to business travel. Over 90 per cent of the total tourists visiting Nepal during the period from 1963 to 1973 came for holiday. Between 1974-1984, the proportion dropped to 80 per cent. It remained slightly above 70 per cent from 1985 to 1991. The decrease in the proportion of tourists was off-set by the increase in trekking and mountaineering. From 1984 onwards, the arrival of tourists for relaxation remained more or less the same with an exception of a drastic fall in 1991.

An appraisal of the tourism sector reveals that it has been an important source of foreign exchange earnings in Nepal. Foreign exchange earnings are shown to be dependent on the number of tourist arrivals, as fluctuations in the number of tourists correlate to the fluctuations in the amount of revenue earned from tourism. The earnings from tourism in the late 80s and early 90s show some increase which is the result of the increase in the exchange rate of foreign currencies compared to the Nepal Rupee.

The number of tourist arrivals are given on the basis of the English calendar while the foreign exchange earnings are computed on a fiscal year basis, which begins on 15 July in Nepal. The growth in the number of hotels, travel and trekking agencies correlates to the number of tourists arriving in Nepal. In the years before 1970, there were several hotels in Kathmandu and only a few in the Chitwan Safari Camps and Pokhara. As there were virtually no travel and trekking agencies, the hotels handled the technicalities of these activities.

But since 1970, the number of tourist arrivals has risen together with the speedy growth in the numbers of hotels, travel agencies and trekking offices. Between 1981 and 1985, a growth in the number of hotels and related service infrastructure has taken place. Ironically, this was also a period when Nepalese tourism did not show any growth in terms of tourist arrivals.

The paradox can be explained by the fact that the development of hotels started in the 1970's when the tourism sector looked encouraging, but due to the highly uncertain nature of tourism, there was a decline in the number of arrivals in ensuing years. The growth of travel and trekking agencies was more rapid. By the end of

1992, 247 travel agencies were registered with the Department of Tourism.

Great importance has been given to tourism development in the Eighth Five Year Plan of Nepal. The plan has laid down specific objectives, policies and programmes for the development of tourism in Nepal. The main objectives are:

1. To expand the tourism industry and tourist activities, which are currently concentrated in only a few areas, by building physical infrastructure and promoting tourism to create additional opportunities for employment. This, in turn, will help ease poverty and raise the standard of living of the population;
2. To increase the number of tourist arrivals;
3. To promote the environmental, historical and cultural heritage and raise the quality of services and facilities related to tourism;
4. To take measures for overseeing the stable development of the tourism industry and link it to other economic sectors in a coordinated manner;
5. To develop the necessary infrastructure for the operation of efficient, safe, comfortable and quality air services for the proper advancement of the tourism industry.

Although concern about environmental degradation started relatively late in Nepal, both the Government and international organizations working in Nepal have strongly acknowledged the problems and recommended measures to balance the environment. Their attention mainly rests on the preservation of endangered wild life fauna, plants and aquatic life and the prevention of further deforestation, which has triggered a host of other problems.

Deforestation aggravates soil erosion and, in so doing, affects the agricultural livelihood of over 80 per cent of the population. It has been an ongoing process that originated long before the advent of tourism in the mid 1960's (Pawsan 1984). Pollution is another alarming problem; it is visible on most routes. Its causes are many and multi-faceted, arising singularly or in combination with several factors such as the following: (a) lack of hygiene, (b) lack of facilities for proper sanitation, particularly for local people, porters and guides, (c) lack of facilities for litter, (d) lack of environmental awareness, (e) ineffective rules and regulations, (f) and lack of monitoring of environmental health.

While deforestation and pollution are the major causes of environmental degradation in the mountains, pollution pressure has not affected the mountains as it has the plains. In the mountains, tourism has become a boon for the survival of local people in terms of providing income for them. On the whole, the tourism sector has generated a living for the locals. However, it has also contributed to the disruption of the environment.

In this light, the trade-off between environmental problems and economic gains created by tourism cannot be measured so easily. A compromise is needed when the economic problems besetting Nepal are considered. Tourism needs to be encouraged, but not without policies to improve and maintain the environment.

Tourists visiting Nepal are not only attracted by the snow peaks, forests, ancient cities and villages but also by the diverse people and cultures of the country. In

Nepal there are 70 ethnic groups who speak roughly 42 different languages. They are separated by geography. People who live in the mountains are different from those who live in the hills or plains (Tarai). They have their own lifestyle, dress, food, religion, ornaments and beliefs. They are traditionally agro-pastoral and are often engaged in business with people in the Tibetan region of China. As such, they are commonly known as Himalayan traders.

Buddhist monks and nuns in culturally rich monasteries and nunneries also reside in the mountains. They live in the unique Himalayan setting of Nepal, where symbiotic relationships among the sacred, secular and eco-sphere prevail. Their firm belief in supernatural forces has made them known worldwide, leaving tourists awed and anxious to make the Himalayan region the prime destination of their visit.

For similar reasons people in the hilly region attracts tourists. Unlike their counterparts in the mountains who subsist on a staple of potato and practice Tibetan Buddhism, the hill people have corn and millet as their staple food. They believe in Hinduism, spirits and shamanism which form additional sources of attraction for tourists.

The southern region of Nepal is mostly inhabited by the Tharus who are no less fascinating than the highlanders or the martial people of the hills. Like the Himalayan region, the Kathmandu Valley is popular with tourists. The Valley possesses all the remnants of ancient and medieval civilizations, providing tourists with a scenario of historical events, beautiful monuments and fine traditions of art.

Here, tourists find a unique religious-cultural blend of Hinduism and Buddhism. They are fascinated with the rituals associated with these religions, such as animal sacrifices, long and arduous pilgrimages, and cremations near the Pasupati Nath Temple. They are also intrigued by the well-preserved material cultural heritage.

Kathmandu is the first destination for the majority of tourists, mainly because Kathmandu is the only city with an international airport. Since over 90 per cent of tourists arrive in Nepal by air, there is no other choice for them. Upon arrival in Kathmandu, the hotels and restaurants provide cultural programmes for tourists. Travel agencies also cater to tourists' needs by providing tours that are conducted by trained city guides.

For more strenuous tourism activities, trekking, mountaineering and rafting expeditions are popular. The Himalayan region offers ample opportunities for tourists who wish to pursue these adventures at their own pace. Trekking in the mountain region falls into three categories: normal trek, controlled trek and guided trek. After trekking, tourists return to either Kathmandu or Pokhara, the second most important destination for tourists, where they set out to do water rafting in the Trisuli River. Rafting in the Sunkosi, Kaligandaki, Arun, Karnali, Bheri and Selikho is also possible.

Aside from trekking, mountaineering and river rafting, a large number of tourists, specially from India, visit Nepal as pilgrims. Indian pilgrims visit holy places that include Pasupatinath in Kathmandu, Gosaikund (a sacred lake in the mountains located in the central region of Nepal associated with the Hindu deity, Shiva), Janakpur, and Lumbini (the birthplace of Lord Buddha). In addition to Indian visitors, there are Japanese, Koreans, Thais. and Sri Lankans who visit Lumbini.

In the Tarai, tourists visit the Chitwan National Park, Bardia National Park, the Kosi Tappu Island and the Royal Shukla Phanta. Because of its ideal location near Kathmandu, the Chitwan National Park is a popular site for tourists. Tourism to these National Parks is popularly known as "wildlife tourism" or "jungle tourism".

Charter of Cultural Tourism

The International Council for Monuments and Sites (ICOMOS) aims to encourage the safeguard and to ensure the conservation and promotion of monuments and sites - that privileged part of the human heritage.In this capacity, it feels directly concerned by the effects - both positive and negative - on said heritage due to the extremely strong development of tourist activities in the world.

ICOMOS is conscious that today - even less than theretofore the isolated effort of any body, however powerful be it in its own sphere, cannot validly influence the course of events. This is why it has attempted to participate in joint reflection with the large world and regional organizations which in one capacity or another share in its preoccupations and which are likely to contribute to the implementation of a universal, coherent and efficacious effort.

The Representatives of these bodies, met in Brussels, Belgium, on 8 and 9 November 1976 at the International Seminar on Contemporary Tourism and Humanism have agreed the following:

Basic Position

1. Tourism is an irreversible social, human, economic and cultural fact. Its influence in the sphere of monuments and sites is particularly important and can but increase because of the known conditions of that activity's development.

2. Looked at in the perspective of the next twenty-five years, in the context of the phenomena of expansion which may have heavy consequences and which confront the human race, tourism appears to be one of the phenomena likely to exert a most significant influence on Man's environment in general and on monuments and sites in particular. In order to remain bearable this influence must be carefully studied, and at all levels be the object of a concerted and effective policy. Without claiming to meet this need in all its aspects, the present approach which is limited to cultural tourism constitutes, it is believed, a positive element in the global solution which is required.

3. Cultural tourism is that form of tourism whose object is, among other aims, the discovery of monuments and sites. It exerts on these last a very positive effect insofar as it contributes - to satisfy its own ends - to their maintenance and protection. This form of tourism justifies in fact the efforts which said maintenance and protection demand of the human community because of the socio-cultural and economic benefits which they bestow on all the populations concerned.

4. Whatever, however, may be its motivations and the ensuing benefits, cultural tourism cannot be considered separately from the negative, despoiling

> or destructive effects which the massive and uncontrolled use of monuments and sites entails. The respect of the latter, just like the elementary wish to maintain them in a state fit to allow them to play their role as elements of touristic attraction and of cultural education, implies the definition and implementation of acceptable standards.

In any case, with the future in mind, it is the respect of the world, cultural and natural heritage which must take precedence over any other considerations however justified these may be from a social, political or economic point of view.

Such respect cannot be ensured solely by policies regarding the siting of equipment and of guidance of the tourist movements based on the limitations of use and of density which may not be disregarded without impunity.

Additionally one must condemn any siting of tourist equipment or services in contradiction with the prime preoccupation due to the respect we owe to the existing cultural heritage.

Basis for Action

Resting on the foregoing,

the bodies representing tourism, on the one hand, and the protection of the natural and monumental heritage, on the other, deeply convinced that the protection and promotion of the natural and cultural heritage for the benefit of the many cannot be ensured unless it be in an orderly fashion, i.e. by integrating cultural assets into the social and economic objectives which are part of planning of the resources of the states, regions and local communities, acknowledge with the greatest interest the measures which each of them states he is prepared to take in his own sphere of influence as expressed in the appendices to the present Declaration,

appeal to the will of the states to ensure the fast and energetic implementation of the International Convention for the Protection of the World Cultural and Natural Heritage adopted on 16 November 1972, and of the Nairobi Recommendation.

trust that the World Tourist Organization, fulfilling its aims, and Unesco in the framework of the Convention mentioned above, shall exert all efforts in cooperation with the signatory bodies and all others who in future may rally to ensure the implementation of the policy which the signatory bodies have defined as the only one able to protect Mankind against the effects of tourism's anarchical growth which would result in the denial of its own objectives.

They express the wish that the states by the means of their administrative structures, of tourist operators' organizations, and users' associations, shall adopt all appropriate measures to facilitate the information and training of persons travelling for tourist purposes inside and out of their country of origin.

Conscious of the acute need which obtains now to change the attitude of the public at large towards the phenomena resulting from the massive development of touristic needs, they express the wish that from school age onwards children and adolescents be educated to understand and respect the monuments, the sites and the cultural heritage and that all written, spoken or visual information media should express to the public the elements of the problem thereby efficaciously contributing to effective universal understanding.

Unanimous in their concern for the protection of the cultural patrimony which is the very basis of international tourism, they undertake to help in the fight initiated on all fronts against the destruction of said heritage by all known sources of pollution; and they appeal to the architects and scientific experts of the whole world so that the most advanced resources of modern technology be used for the protection of monuments.

They recommend that the specialists who shall be called upon to conceive and implement the touristic use of the cultural and the natural heritage should receive training adapted to the multi-faceted nature of the problem, and should be associated from the outset in the programming and performance of the development and tourist equipment plans.

They solemnly declare that their action is to respect and protect the authenticity and diversity of the cultural values in developing regions and countries as in industrialized nations since the fate of Mankind's cultural heritage is of the very same nature everywhere in the face of tourism's likely expansion.

3

Adventure Tourism

The term 'adventure' is an experience of some sort, providing a level of personal excitement. What to one person may simply be a common occupation or sporting activity, may to another, be unique and exciting. It can therefore be a matter of degree and personal opinion. The Oxford Dictionary refers to adventure as an exciting experience, a risk or enterprising activity. Adventure tourism is activity-based with a distinction between hard and soft adventure tourism:

— Hard adventure tourism introduces tourists to natural outdoor settings, engages them in a variety of activities in a challenging environment where risk taking is the key motivation.

— Soft adventure tourism is exciting and is often educational and discovery, the environment, heritage and indigenous culture are common aspects and guided tours are frequently the medium by which tourists achieve that experience.

There is no commonly agreed profile of an adventure tourist as adventure tourism embraces a broadrange of motivational characteristics, risk, excitement, educational and aesthetic appreciation. Nevertheless some characteristics of an adventure tourist appear in adventure tourism literature and suggest they are affluent, well-educated, having an interest in environmental issues, traditional cultures and remote or difficult destinations. The literature highlights special interest in adventure tourism by women generally, women travelling solo and as seniors.

Women constitute the dominant market for packaged, overnight, commercial adventure tourism and typically comprise more than 60 per cent of all participants. By contrast, non-commercial outdoor recreation is dominated by men. An American adventure company operator suggests:

"People just don't want to go and sit by a beach any more. They want to do something and they want to achieve something when they go on holiday. "She also believes that adventure travel in Australia will become as big as in the US where researchers predict that ageing baby boomers, the health and fitness trend and a "backlash against electronic isolation" will fuel the professionals' search for thrills for years.

Adventure travel is already a US $300 billion industry in the US and according to US research, most adventure travellers are well-educated, baby boomers, many of them women. As the definition suggests, Adventure Tourism encompasses a broad range of activities. Due to its diversity, this niche sector can impact upon other sectors such as sports tourism, nature based tourism, ecotourism, special events and indigenous tourism.

Adventure can be a matter of interpretation or opinion. It is always an experience of some sort but providing excitement. What to one person may be a common or mundane activity, may to another, be exciting. Therefore the range of Adventure Tourism products is sufficiently broad as to include businesses that may well be unaware that there are aspects of those businesses that are tourism related, due to their principal activity being for other purposes.

The activities that could be included in the Adventure Tourism niche may also fall into other sectors. While many locations around Australia and overseas offer adventure experiences, there is very little creation of an identifiable sector, collective marketing nor a single point to arrange an Adventure tourism experience. Adventure Tourism is an emerging niche market and shows potential to be very popular and high yielding.

Adventure Tourism represents one of the fastest growing market segments of today's travel market, with its popularity having grown significantly in the last two decades. According to the president of the US Adventure Travel Society, adventure tourism is growing at a rate of 8 per cent per year and generated US $200 billion in 1996. The Australian Tourist Commission (ACT) reports on the US market: "Ageing baby boomers reject tradition. Baby boomers are moving into the 'senior travel' category with a twist – they're not interested in typical 'senior' activities."

Adventure travel has been one of the fastest growing sectors of European tourism over the last few years, albeit from a very small base. The sector is not well documented in Europe, yet evidence suggests that adventure travel from major European markets has increased by around 15 per cent annually since 1995 – way ahead of increases in mainstream tourism.

Australia-wide, various operators cater for the adventure tourism market. Some of the operators which provide or focus on adventure travel include Raging Thunder, AAT Kings, Contiki. Reviewing the tours that these operators offer, none makes mention of the ACT as a possible destination. These tour operators largely offer tours in the Northern Territory Outback and national parks, the Queensland cities, coast and the Great Barrier Reef including islands as well as the tropical rainforest, Tasmanian national parks and coast, Western Australian coast, forests, national parks and desert and the New South Wales Blue Mountains.

There is evidence that the destinations as well as the businesses work closely together with the tour operators that are highly integrated with roof organisations such as travel agents. The market for Adventure Tourism is on our doorstep. Canberra has a young population with a higher than average disposable income, a higher than average employment rate, seeking new and exciting experiences. It must be made recognisable and easy to reach. In addition to the local market, the more populated area of Sydney has potential as a market within reasonable reach of Canberra.

International visitors are generally high yield. It appears they look for well-developed adventure tourism opportunities. The ACT can combine that with experiencing the Australian bush and many other Canberra attractions.

Canberra's neighbours in the national capital region, offer snow activities, mountaineering, sea kayaking, deep-sea fishing and sailing, run by business people operating out of Canberra and within the region. A brilliant way to do sightseeing in Canberra is out of a hot air balloon. Admire the perfect design of Canberra from a bird's perspective while the sun rises over the picturesque mountain ranges of the Brindabellas. For real adventure seekers, paragliding, parachuting or tandem hang gliding forms part of the agenda. The rivers Murrumbidgee, Cotter, Goodradigbee and Upper Murray run through Canberra surrounds and offer excellent whitewater rafting possibilities for starters as well as for an advanced level.

However, the ACT domestic adventure travel industry is in its infancy. Many involved are part time due to the markets they serve (mainly weekend visitors) and the relatively undeveloped state of the industry. A number of mostly small businesses, catering to small groups of people provide a range of specialist adventure/travel/vacation experiences. Adventure tour operators in the ACT appear to have a modest understanding of the needs, wants and desires of their clients.

Moreover there is no roof organisation distributing and marketing the ACT adventure tourism product and there seems to be a lack of communication and joint forces between the parties involved in adventure tourism.

Tourism experiences to visitors who are here for other reasons such as to visit museums and galleries or attending conferences and conventions. They can be offered a very memorable experience while in Canberra. As pointed out before, more that 100 regional tour operators have a direct link to Adventure Tourism. However, the range of activities in adventure tourism is so broad as to include businesses that may be unaware that aspects of them are tourism related, due to their principal activity being for other purposes.

Examples which demonstrate Adventure Tourism has something to offer a business or presents a new perspective for a business, might be:

— The light aircraft operator at the Airport says he is in the transport sector. He is correct. But if he can also run joy flights and skydiving he is in adventure tourism too.

— The retailer who sells/hires clothing and sports items for recreational activities is also involved in adventure tourism, in equipping people for the adventure they are about to experience. That retailer may also take bookings for rafting, canoeing or skiing.

— The backpacker hostels are in the accommodation business. Backpackers are one of the greatest single sources of adventure-seeking tourists. A hostel will benefit from adventure seeking tourists, as also will adventure tourism operators benefit from the backpacker hostel's guests. The strength of a group with over 100 operators, working collectively can provide a huge product base, great collective marketing prospects and an ability to draw a range of visitors from many markets.

While there are important environmental considerations to be observed, particularly when operating outdoors, many activities can be conducted safely and well when environmental safeguards are observed. Adventure Tourism is an excellent opportunity to have tourists embrace the environment and learn about their sensitivities and become environmental protection champions themselves.

A businesses which might easily be identified as being associated with adventure tourism: The diversity of adventure tourism can be seen when realising all sectors that impinge upon this niche market include:

— Backpackers and low cost accommodation
— Bus companies
— Clubs (universities, social, sports, etc, of various types)
— Educators (through personal development courses)
— Foundations (via personal development courses) eg., Outward Bound, Duke of Edinbourough Scheme
— Indigenous interpretation and experiences
— Light aircraft and helicopter operators
— Motor home and caravan rental
— Nature and national park operations
— Pilot training
— Sheep and cattle property owners
— Sports clothing suppliers
— Sports equipment suppliers
— Sports goods suppliers
— Team building courses
— Tour operators
— Venue operator/owners
— Behavioural problem remedial therapy
— Backpackers
— Events

— Indigenous

— Nature based / ecotourism

— Retail

— Sport

— Transport

Adventure Tourism is an exciting, rapidly growing segment of the international tourism industry. This new sector is a result of major changes in consumer preference and lifestyle. Activities in the adventure tourism sector can be grouped under two main headings: those that fall into the "consumptive sector", like hunting and fishing; and those in the "non-consumptive" sector.

The non-consumptive adventure tourism industry includes two classes of experiences:

— *Hard adventure:* ocean kayaking, whitewater canoeing, and expedition-style backpacking and ski-touring.

— *Soft adventure:* bicycle touring with van support, day hiking, nature and culture viewing, sail touring, and boat tours.

Global and National perspective:

> Globally, tourism is valued at approximately $2 trillion. Nationally, the industry produces revenue of $25 billion. Given the longer retirement periods and relative affluence of many North American and European individuals, it is expected that tourism will experience substantial growth over the next decade.

Newfoundland and Labrador Perspective:

> Non-resident tourist trips and expenditures in Newfoundland and Labrador have increased steadily

> since 1991. It is expected that many non-resident travelers in the future will be seeking adventure type vacations, resulting in even more trips and expenditures in the province.

Adventure tourism has the potential to add significantly to the province's tourism industry through expansion of the consumptive hunting and fishing sector, and by attracting the non-consumptive tourist who appreciates the province's environmental advantages.

In Newfoundland and Labrador today, tourism is responsible for an estimated 15,000 direct jobs. Expenditures in all parts of the tourism sector, by residents and non-residents combined, are more than $500 million dollars. Tourism is a major part of our province's economy.

Major investments continue to be made in the tourism sector to ensure that the province's attractions and services deliver a quality tourism experience. The civic centres in St. John's and Corner Brook will deliver many new, high-yield conventions to the province. New interpretation centres, such as the Grenfell Centre in St. Anthony, make the province's culture and history more accessible. New snowmobile trails will add to the province's growing array of winter tourism activities, which now include nordic and alpine skiing, heli-skiing and cat-skiing.

Adventure tourism has been singled out as an opportunity for growth because of the province's abundance of unparalleled beauty and natural resources. Newfoundland and Labrador's main competitive advantages lie in the quality of their vast accessible wilderness, coastline, and clean inland waters.

Opportunities for growth exist in both consumptive and non-consumptive activities.

The province is comprised of more than 400,000 square kilometers of greatly varied terrain that is home to diverse species of fish and game. This diversity has given Newfoundland and Labrador a well-established reputation as a paradise for sports fishers and big game hunters.

Wildlife populations including moose, black bears and caribou are thriving. The province is well positioned to take advantage of increased consumptive sector opportunities. The majority of established adventure tourism employers in the province operate in the consumptive sector.

Although the non-consumptive component now accounts for less than 10% of world tourism, it is the fastest growing portion of the industry with an annual growth rate of approximately 30%. Non-consumptive tourism has great potential in Newfoundland and Labrador. Currently, approximately 56 businesses are operating in the non-consumptive sector.

Preparation required for working in this industry involves locating businesses which provide employment opportunities of interest. It is then important to consider the occupations of people working in those areas. Although this industry offers growth opportunities, certain occupational areas may not offer high employment potential. It is important to check occupational descriptions for employment projections. Thousands of occupational areas are available for people to explore. The following list outlines a relatively small number of occupations that may relate to the industry.

Tourism was not discussed when the Antarctic Treaty was negotiated in 1959. The Protocol on Environmental Protection to the Antarctic Treaty, concluded in 1991, set out rules that apply to any impact on the Antarctic Environment. In recent year concerns have been raised about the increase in Adventure Tourism to Antarctica.

Since the formation of IAATO there is now reliable recording of individuals, groups and companies traveling to Antarctica. Member companies are required to provide information on all activities within Antarctica on an annual basis.

Additionally IAATO has been extremely pro active in securing as much information as possible on the non-IAATO members and their plans for current seasons. This allows IAATO to follow the trends in Antarctic tourism and the diversity of new and unusual activities. While recent reports show optional pursuits such as kayaking, camping and climbing may now be available on selected voyages there is as yet no indication that these new ventures have had any detrimental impact on the Antarctic environment.

Ship base Adventure Tourism

Over the last 5 years activities available aboard and from a cruise vessel have expanded and been developed to accomodate new and active travelers. Of those participating in these ventures, the majority tends to be small numbers of passengers, traveling with reputable companies who have experience in a particular sport or the appropriate and qualified staff to facilitate.

All additional tours operated by IAATO members are assèssed in advance for safety, have secured the required permits and compliances and in the event of an accident or emergency are covered by the company's insurance policies.

It should be noted that the number of passengers participating in these Adventure programs account for less than 0.5% of all tourists traveling to Antarctica. The number is relatively small and to date there is no documentation to suggest there is any adverse impact on the environment by or from these programs.

Land Based Adventure Tourism

Living in a tent at minus 15°C for 2 weeks to reach a destination on the polar plateau will for most people be considered extreme and adventurous. However, one of the IAATO member companies has been operating and taking tourists to this extreme environment for 16 consecutive seasons. They believe that with the lessons they have drawn over their years of operation that they are in a position to offer safe and responsible tourism to the interior of Antarctica.

They consider themselves self sufficient without reliance on any of the National Operators or their equipment though work closely with many of the National Operators throughout the Antarctic season. More recently there have been a sporadic number of private expeditions wishing to reach/cross/visit Antarctica without any support, back up or insurance.

These groups have any detrimental effect on the Antarctic environment. The greater concern is the effect an emergency, accident or incident may have on tour companies or National Operators. These groups are cause for greater concern as there is no way of knowing where they are going, what they are doing, if they have all the necessary permit and insurance and if their experience is appropriate for an Antarctic Journey.

In short, we believe that there is a place in Antarctica for Adventure Tourism. It may be the modern adaptation of the journeys we have offered for almost 40 years. We need however to ensure that it is responsible tourism and is governed by the same criteria and parameters applied to all current tourists and National Operators traveling to Antarctica.

They must secure all the required permits, show appropriate insurance cover for emergency and environmental situations, back up for search and rescue for the duration of their time in Antarctica and an access and exit plan. We must agree that those parties taking them to Antarctica are responsible for them until their return from Antarctica. There needs to be a penalty for those choosing to ignore these requirements. Antarctic will not care whether a person paying to be there or being paid to be there creates the damage.

Global Market of Adventure Tourism

Nature and adventure travel is primarily a niche market where over the last decade, there has been significant growth. It has been estimated for example that outbound adventure travel from Europe has increased by around 15 percent per annum since 1995 and a similar trend has appeared with the North American markets. The European and North American markets account for the majority of the world's nature and adventure travellers.

Some of the distinguishing trends in nature and adventure travel over the last 10 to 20 years include:

— Growing awareness and concern for the environment coupled with a dramatic increase in areas being managed for nature/adventure or ecotourism;

— Increased profile of nature and adventure travel via the internet, TV (Sky Sport, Discovery Channel), commercial nature and adventure magazines such as Action Asia, New Zealand Adventure;

— Specialisation of outbound and inbound nature/adventure tour operators;

— High cost group adventure travel by the over 40 year olds, with many in the 60+ age group;

— FIT adventure travel by the younger 25 - 40 year olds;

— A proliferation of outdoor clothing and equipment manufacturers and retailers;

— Growth in global, multi-million dollar outdoor adventure races (Eco-Challenge, Raid Gauloise, Camel Trophy);

— Growth in both 'soft-adventure' (nature walks) and 'hard adventure' (climbing Everest) with a noticeable trend towards 'roughing it';

— Improved safety standards and professionalism of nature/adventure operators, including the formation of professional industry associations and accreditation programmes (for instance, PADI, UIAGM, NEAP);

— Increasing supply of nature and adventure travel companies has meant that loyalty to brands is constantly shifting;

— Increased legislation, policy and regulation of the nature and adventure sector.

Some adventure markets have become multidisciplinary, wanting a combination of activities such as mountain biking and sea kayaking, sailing and diving, trekking and rafting. This is very true of the younger FITs, who have grown up with the boom in the diversity of leisure activities during the 1980s and 1990s, but to a certain extent this trend is also affected by the destination. For example, locations such as Vava'u, Tonga, can offer sailing and diving, sea kayaking, whale watching and mountain biking, so too can Queenstown, New Zealand, where bungy jumping, rafting, jet boating and skiing are often undertaken during a single visit.

However, not all destinations have a range of complementary activities on offer. Other nature and adventure markets, particularly noticeable with older age groups, have developed a strong focus on single activity tours such as trekking in Nepal, natural history tours to Niue or nature and wildlife cruises to the Antarctic and Sub Antarctic Islands. Social and economic factors underpin many of these trends. Since the 1950s, participation in outdoor leisure activities has not only exploded, it has become increasingly commercialised.

The populations of North America, Europe, Australia and New Zealand are reportedly ageing but in general have more wealth, outdoor skill and experience than ever before. Environmental awareness has been stimulated by TV, internet, popular articles and education systems. The result is that nature/adventure markets are generally well travelled and very particular about safety, environmental 'best practice' and standards of service. With increasing ease in world travel, visitors can also compare products both within and between regions. For example, similar FIT nature/adventure markets can be found in Fiji and Indonesia, the Cook Islands and Thailand.

Most of the global trends mentioned are evident in the South Pacific. A key question to consider is how to manage, build on or take advantage of the trends. The 2000 Camel Trophy was a good example of how the South Pacific benefited from an international adventure event and we suspect more of these types of activities will enter the region over the next decade. The latest World Tourism Organisation's (WTO) forecast for the East Asia and Pacific region predicts that tourism will continue to grow at an annual average growth rate of 6.5 percent to 2020. Coupled with other popular statistics that state that nature, adventure or eco-type travel has been the fastest growing sector world wide and you could assume that the development of nature and adventure products in the South Pacific is in for a good time over the next two decades.

Certainly there has been growth in nature and adventure products in the South Pacific, but not all of the operators in this sector would say it has been commercially successful. The reasons for this vary with the motivations for entering the sector in the first place. Some big game fishermen have set up charters as a semi-retirement business. Others, like the Vatthe Conservation Area on Espiritu Santo, got into guided nature walks and bird watching as a means to protect their forest and generate a bit of income for the village. Those such as Cutting Edge Adventures in Vanuatu, Adventures in Paradise in Fiji, the Friendly Islands Kayak Company and some of the whale watch operators in Vava'u appear clearly focused on building a strong business with local partners. This is fairly typical of most niche markets. They develop when dedicated specialists convert their passion for an activity into a business enterprise. The result is often a mixed story of success as the transition from outdoor enthusiast to business person is not that easy.

Marine products dominate nature and adventure activities in the South Pacific although over the last five to 10 years, there has been growth in the number of land-based products.

Swimming, snorkelling and short walks (non-guided) have already been put forward as the most popular nature-based activities in the South Pacific. The second most popular marine activity is scuba diving and this looks set to remain one of the most popular adventure activities given the growth in diving in the South Pacific's key source markets (US, Australia, New Zealand, UK/Europe). There are specialised outbound dive agents in New Zealand, Australia and around 15 - 20 in the US. Significant growth has occurred with sea kayaking over the last five years. Some, like Cutting Edge Adventures in Vanuatu are based in-country, whilst others such as Friendly Islands Sea Kayak Company and Tamarillo Sea Kayaks are based in New Zealand and move to Vava'u and Fiji respectively to run trips during the April - November season.

There are limited wholesalers or agents who specialise in this area and so some sea kayak operators get almost all of their bookings directly via email, internet or 'snail mail'. Growth has and is occurring in both day and overnight trips. Windsurfing is even more specialised with only one operator in Fiji and one in New Caledonia who offer windsurfing packages. Another niche activity is surfing and in Samoa, this activity has grown from around 20 surfers in the early 1990s to around 1,000 surfers in 2000. Reef breaks and strong currents makes the South Pacific suitable for only the most experienced surfers.

Fishing is available throughout the South Pacific and apart from a small US bone fishing market in Kiribati, the markets are quite diverse. Whilst the popular destinations include Tonga, Vanuatu, Fiji and the Solomon Islands, many big game fishing operations find it a difficult business to be in. Big game charters are expensive and require minimum numbers and long days to make it worthwhile. The size of this market is small compared with the market for two - three hour fishing excursions for families or non-fishers who are keen to try their hand. The latter market is not really catered for in the South Pacific yet it appears to offer good opportunities, particularly for local people to own and run their own business.

Land based activities such as guided walks to waterfalls, caves, forests and so on have grown steadily over the last decade. The successful tour operators are those who are linked with local accommodation, have strong networks with the NTO and in some cases, offshore wholesalers but importantly, they provide professional guides who are good at interpreting their natural and cultural history.

Overnight trekking is a small niche area that is emerging in Fiji, PNG, the Cook Islands and Vanuatu. Overnight or two night/three day treks are more popular than longer trips and like the successful day tour operations, the overnight operations that combine good interpretation with a safe, professional trekking service are keeping ahead of the rest of the field.

The nature and adventure markets in the South Pacific tend to be dominated by visitors from the US, Australia, New Zealand, UK and West European countries. There are those in this audience who know more about the markets than we do, but we have noticed that within and spread across these countries are a number of possible segments which are worth discussing here:

Adventure Travellers - sometimes misleadingly referred to as backpackers, this market is typically aged 25 - 40 years old, well educated and are either having a break from study or are in professional occupations. Their spending capacity ranges from the 'totally budget conscious' to those that will 'stay cheap' but spend money on a two tank dive, overnight trek or other quality outdoor activity. They are information hungry, use email or the internet before leaving on holiday and the Lonely Planet guidebook whilst on holiday.

Adventure travellers move around the Pacific, often on part of a longer holiday to Australia or New Zealand. Dominant markets are from the US, UK, Germany, Switzerland and the Netherlands. They had a strong presence in Fiji prior to the May 2000 Coup but also have a preference for Samoa, the Cook Islands and to a lesser extent, Tonga. They use word of mouth referrals as a way of finding out about quality tours and budget places to stay and eat.

Divers - typically in good employment, aged 25 - 50 and often travel on group dive packages (especially the US dive market). For those on decompression dives, there is normally one day free where they will participate in non-dive activities such as a coastal walk, village visits, fishing trip, mountain biking or a kayak trip. Special interest - whilst divers could be described as special interest it is the share size of the dive market, that makes it worth singling out. Special interest visitors could be grouped according to their specific activities, for instance, sea kayakers, yachties, bird watchers and ecotourists and surfers. Each have their own particular characteristics which will not be explored here, suffice to say they are visiting the South Pacific primarily because of a single activity or interest. There is a lack of detailed market intelligence about these visitors although there is evidence that each activity is showing growth.

General Packaged South Pacific Holiday - this group is characterised by first-time visitors, aged 40 - 60+ with limited outdoor skills but who will go on a waterfall walk, day hike, snorkel tour or boat trip to explore outer islands. In terms of marketing, the obvious trends in the nature and adventure sector could be · listed as:

— A major shift towards direct marketing via email, internet and editorials;

— Increasing use of joint marketing (especially backpacker accommodation);

— Wider use of travel media with editorials in special interest magazines (for instance New Zealand Fishing News, Adventure, US Diver magazines);

— Reliance on word-of-mouth;

— Ongoing use of the Lonely Planet, Pacific Handbook and other similar guidebooks;

— Use of specialist wholesalers or agents (for instance, for all-inclusive diving, surfing, sailing, fishing and windsurfing packages).

These trends imply that marketing a nature or adventure product in the South Pacific is a 'horses for courses' situation. There is no single formula that will suit every product. The special interest markets, for instance the windsurfers and multi-day sea kayakers, are pre-booked, often via email or internet web site. There is little need for those operators to advertise locally, unless they wish to encourage walk-in business. There is certainly talk of less reliance on wholesalers by those operators who market their product directly. However, some of these operators will also tell you what a hassle it can be replying to each and every email request from booked clients who just love that level of personal attention. On balance, that is not a bad trade-off against a 15 - 20 percent commission.

On the other hand, the dug-out canoe tour of the Sanaapu-Sataoa mangrove in Samoa, the Vidawa Rainforest Hike on Taveuni, Fiji or Misa's Forest Walk in Niue have no need to bother with internet or email. They operate best by having a good mention in the Lonely Planet guide, brochures or flyers with the NTO and nearby accommodation and if fortunate, would have had a feature article in an in-flight magazine or other nature/ adventure publication in a source country (possibly facilitated by the NTOs travel media programme).

There is ongoing concern however about how far the industry should go with offering FOCs to media. It has been suggested that overall, more careful screening is required before offering FOCs particularly to media outside the main source markets. In summary, an FOC to a big, established operator may not be that significant but FOCs to a small to medium sized operation, can cause a serious dent in the cash flow. Whilst operators have to focus on building their own business within each South Pacific destination, it will be interesting see when or if these businesses try to jointly market themselves on a regional basis. The other likely scenario is that once an operator gets established in one destination, it is tempting to set-up elsewhere, thereby establishing a regional profile.

South Pacific has at least one 'signature' product and a range of others that have and can position the South Pacific as a serious nature and adventure destination. Examples include the Pentacost land dive in Vanuatu, diving throughout the region, sea kayaking and whale watching. The issue to consider is how these products can be strengthened and positioned in the source markets. Copy-cat operators abound in the South Pacific and competition is tough. Whilst some strong products stand out (diving, sailing, some fishing operations, sea kayaking and snorkelling), there appears an oversupply of scenic tours, waterfall walks and cave trips and yet there is a perception in some markets that there is still not enough to see and do.

The South Pacific has a strong image of an island paradise. The level of awareness that the region can also offer quality nature and adventure is relatively low in source markets but appears to be improving as new products are developed. The match between image and reality is crucial to nature and adventure clients and we need to learn from past mistakes. There appears to be plenty of opportunity to seek out creative ways to integrate nature and adventure products into current destination brand images.

The South Pacific Regional Tourism Marketing Plan makes a point worth recording here in that... 'if presented as a destination for the adventurous traveller who is willing to "explore and discover", expectations will be pitched more accurately for the realities and frustrations of travel in the South Pacific.' While the Plan goes onto state that long haul markets will pay well to visit unspoiled and remote locations, we have direct experience that suggests demand from the Australian and New Zealand markets should not be underestimated.

Generally, there is a shortage of local expertise for running nature and adventure tourism activities. Whilst there are talented Fijian divers, Tongan whale watching guides and so on, the issue is further complicated by the introduction of white, Western style activities (sea kayaking, windsurfing, big game fishing, sailing), many of which require significant capital investment and technical expertise not commonly available in the South Pacific. Rightly or wrongly, the result has been that the nature and adventure tourism sector in the South Pacific is dominated by palagis. It is a sensitive issue but if we take an 'us and them' approach, it will only get worse.

There are good Pacific Island role models (divers, sea kayak guides, forest guides) who have an 'I can do this too' attitude and it would be great to raise their profile to inspire others who wish to enter or get ahead in this sector. Skilled guides who can tell the stories of their natural and cultural history are in strong demand from the European and North American nature and adventure markets. Furthermore, training opportunities are available, especially through donor agencies such as NZODA and AusAID. If we think back 10 years, the skill base was a lot less than what it is today and we should feel positive about this achievement.

A small number of nature and adventure operators are making a comfortable living whilst many are finding that the financial returns are not as good as they expected. In general, there has been a lack of detailed business plans or feasibility studies undertaken before the start-up phase. Passion, an important ingredient for success, is not likely to be enough on its own. Many of the region's community ecotourism ventures are not financially viable and simple business principles are not being taken seriously. Overlying this are pressures from traditional forms of giving such as faalave lave, kerekere and faka Tonga on small businesses. Many small operators complain about the lack of start-up capita' and banks are taking a harder line on lending.

Whilst some of these are unlikely to change (for instance, kerekere), we all have the ability to take simple business principles more seriously. In a Pacific context, the nature and adventure tourism sector presents an important opportunity for indigenous communities or individuals to own and run a small business. The two main issues here involve a lack of start-up capital and the ability to match the size of the market demand with the size of the business and the dedicated skills and lifestyle of the operator.

The nature and adventure markets already described are discerning, often well travelled and in the case of special interest groups, are very particular about what they want. They will quickly turn to other destinations and operators if they cannot get what was promised. Honesty with the marketing, making sure that the images are in-line with what gets delivered, is very important. Further to this, we see that operators who start with one clear product and make it the best available at the destination, will often have a leading edge over others. Copy-cats often cannot compete with those who were first into the market with a good product. The lesson 'start small and get it right' stands out for us.

Running any business is hard work and doing it in the South Pacific has its share of additional worries (air access, political instability, seasonality, cyclones and so on). Those operators who have kept borrowings to a minimum and who have tested the market first, have managed to ride out the lean off-seasons and disruptions with air access.

Nature and adventure markets are typically small and specialised, therefore operators must be equally small, specialised, and flexible. Ironically, this requires the operator to be more professional than many larger businesses because this sort of activity cannot afford to buy the specialist expertise and suffer the inevitable flabbiness that comes with larger businesses.

4

Leisure Tourism

Tourism plays an important role in the national economy and in the prosperity of many cities, towns and rural areas. As well as the annual family holiday tourism also includes a wide range of shorter visits, day trips and short or weekend breaks. It includes travel for business as well as for recreation.

The leisure and tourism industries provide a variety of activities for people to enjoy in their leisure time. The industries are made up of many different facilities and organisations, from leisure centres and theatres to travel agents and airlines. Leisure and tourism industries are linked and how businesses work together to offer visitors a good service.

Tourism destinations are places that people choose to visit and where they spend their leisure time. The travel and tourism industry provides products and services for people who wish to visit these destinations. The popular tourism destinations including:

— where they are

— what they offer visitors

— the main transport routes to them.

Leisure can be described as embracing the entire range of activities that individuals undertake in their free time. Leisure is one of the fastest-growing industries in the UK. People are always looking for new ways to spend their leisure time. That leisure activities are many and varied, and include activities such as:

— reading;

— sport - participating and spectating;

— going to the cinema or a disco;

— going for a walk;

— watching television or listening to the radio;

— eating out;

— playing computer games;

— visiting a tourist attraction.

Since the term 'leisure' covers an enormous range of activities and facilities in a wide variety of situations, it is useful to divide the leisure industry into a number of key components. The key components are:

— sport and physical recreation, eg hockey, football and gymnastics;

— arts and entertainment, eg theatres, cinemas, night-clubs;

— countryside recreation, eg walking, cycling;

— home-based leisure, eg watching TV, gardening, DIY, computer games;

— children's play activities, eg adventure playgrounds and play schemes;

— visitor attractions, eg historic buildings and sites, theme parks and leisure parks;

— catering, eg pubs, cafes, restaurants.

In any area there will be a variety of organisations and facilities that fit into each of these components. How leisure provision meets the needs of different people in an area and how this provision has changed in the last twenty years.

These components are often interrelated. For example, horse riding can be classed as both a sport and a countryside recreation activity. The leisure industry has grown to meet people's leisure needs made up of a wide range of facilities, for example:

— leisure centres and health clubs;

— libraries;

— video-rental shops;

— cinemas and theatres;

— pubs, restaurants and take-away restaurants;

— community centres;

— museums and galleries;

— sports venues;

— theme parks.

Leisure facilities provided at the local level should be studied. are: leisure centres, health clubs, swimming pools, sports grounds, parks and gardens, libraries, country parks, museums and galleries, theatres and cinemas, restaurants and public houses.

The leisure facilities provide a range of products and services. For example, a leisure centre might provide:

— sports activities;

— lessons and classes for different groups of people;

— functions;

— food and drink;

— special rates for members and/or groups;

— purchase and hire of equipment.

The choices that people make about how to enjoy their leisure time may be influenced by many factors, including:

— age group;

— culture;

— special needs;

— type of household, for example families, single people, couples;

— gender;

— social group.

The other factors that affect what people choose to do in their leisure time. These include:

— the availability of local facilities;

— the availability of transport;

— their interests;

— fashion;

— the influence of family and friends;

— how much money they have to spend on leisure.

Few industries can match the leisure industry for the range of employment opportunities it offers.

Tourism is a broad area to define but it usually covers temporary travel (at least one night away) from home or work. An essential part of tourism is the traveller's intention to return home afterwards. The purpose of visits include:

— a holiday;

— sightseeing;

— visiting an attraction;

— visiting friends or relatives;

— going to a sports event as a spectator or to participate;

— business.

Since the term 'travel and tourism' covers an enormous range of activities in a wide variety of situations, it is useful to divide the industry into key components. The key components are:

— travel agents;

— tour operators;

— tourist information and guiding services;

— on-line travel services;

— accommodation and catering;

— attractions;

— transportation.

The following methods of travel by which people get to their chosen destination and how they travel around the area they are visiting. Their relative merits, in terms of cost, convenience and availability:

— air;

— rail;

— sea;

— road.

The social, economic and environmental impact of tourism on at least two of these destinations and how they may be developed in a sustainable manner.

The travel and tourism industry consists of a wide variety of organisations of different sizes and offers many employment opportunities. You will need to know about the range of types of jobs, for example:

— travel consultants;

— conference organisers;

— coach drivers;

— air cabin crew;

— tourist guide;

— resort representative.

Although the leisure and tourism industries are generally considered separately, there are many links between the two, for example accommodation and catering, attractions, and transportation. Both industries are dependent upon each other for customers, for example:

— a family day out at a visitor attraction is a leisure activity but also involves travel and tourism;

— travelling to an away football match could be considered as both leisure and tourism;

— going on holiday and many of the activities undertaken while on holiday could be considered as both leisure and tourism;

— going to the theatre and staying in a hotel overnight are both leisure and tourism.

The local tourist information centre provides details of both leisure and tourism facilities and activities. Transport providers operate services to places of interest for both the leisure market and tourists.

Centres should focus as much as possible on the operation and management of these organisations and the business environment in which they exist. It is also implied that candidates will be required to gain an understanding of how the leisure and tourism industries operate at both the local and national scales. Many centres will choose to study the leisure industry as it is represented in the local area but leisure facilities that are significant at the national scale should also be studied.

Centres should also appreciate that the tourism component of the qualification is more concerned with inbound than outbound tourism. Although the roles of travel agents, tour operators etc should be covered, the primary focus should relate to tourism destinations and the infrastructure that supports them. Candidates need to gain an understanding of the range of tourism destinations and why they appeal to different groups of people - including overseas visitors.

Although it is convenient to treat leisure and tourism as separate industries, in reality there are complex links between them and centres should be encouraged to illustrate to candidates the nature of these links. There are a number of examples where organisations operate within both industries and where the products and services provided by the leisure industry complement those provided by the tourism industry.

The terms such as, for example, these include and including are used to indicate that the lists are not definitive. Candidates should be encouraged to consider the concept of leisure and the use of leisure time. Candidates need to become familiar with the concept that the leisure industry is divided into a number of key components.

It would be good practice for centres to investigate how each of the key components is represented in the local area by organisations and facilities. As indicated in the 'what you need to learn' section of the unit, the full range of leisure facilities provided at the local level should be investigated. Some of these facilities will provide for home-based leisure.

Where resources allow, visits could be made to leisure and tourism organisations in different components to investigate the products and services they provide.

New leisure activities are now available, e.g. computer games, certain traditional activities have increased in popularity e.g. cycling, certain lifestyles have become popular leading to increased provision of health and fitness facilities, DIY stores and so on, health and fitness equipment is more sophisticated, new sports have emerged e.g. skateboarding, major sports have become multi-million pound industries and the relationship between the public and private sectors regarding the provision of leisure facilities has become more complex.

Candidates could investigate the ways in which aspects of the changing provision of leisure activities has changed in recent years or could study the recent changes within a particular activity. It is important that candidates appreciate that there is an extensive range of facilities that provide for the leisure needs of different groups of people. In addition, candidates will need to be clear about the functions of various facilities and be aware of the differences between galleries and museums, leisure centres and health clubs, and so on.

It is important that candidates appreciate that the differences between products and services provided by leisure and tourism organisations are both many and varied. Leisure and tourism products can be both tangible and intangible. For many facilities, the range of products and services offered may be much wider than the candidate might imagine and case studies of local facilities can be used to exemplify this.

The example of a leisure centre in the unit could be contrasted with a hotel that offers meals, conference facilities, banqueting facilities, wedding receptions, weekend dinner dances and other products as well as providing accommodation. This would be a good example of a facility providing different components and operating in both the leisure and tourism industries. The choices available to different groups of people regarding how they spend their leisure time should also be considered. Participation in various leisure activities is dependant on a number of social, economic and geographical factors that could be investigated.

A number of strategies can be used to investigate the patterns of leisure activities undertaken by groups of candidates, however it is vitally important that candidates gain an appreciation of the leisure interests of other groups and that the leisure industry provides products and services for all of these groups.

Leisure facilities can be investigated to obtain information about the range of products and services they provide for different groups of people, including those with special needs. Additionally, candidates should have an appreciation of the range of special needs that different groups will have. Only a small number of the many jobs available within the leisure industry are referred.

Candidates should have some appreciation of the range of other jobs available and be aware of the skills and personal qualities required as well as some understanding of the nature of the work involved. Centres should help candidates to become aware of the scope of travel and tourism and the significance of business travel as opposed to leisure travel should examined.

As with the components of the leisure industry, examples of the components of the travel and tourism industry present within the local area can be used as case studies. Those components that also occur within the leisure industry could be identified and discussed. There may be value in examining the relationships between travel agents and tour operators. Both travel agents and tour operators operate exclusively within the private sector whereas tourist information is usually provided by public sector organisations.

The Internet has led to a revolution in the way holidays and travel can be researched and booked. All destinations now have websites; airlines, hotels and other travel service providers now operate on-line booking systems. A variety of travel and tourism organisations could be investigated by navigating their web-sites.

Candidates should be aware of the terminology associated with holidays and should be able to provide definitions. Resources such as holiday brochures can be used to exemplify the different types available. Candidates will need to be aware of the merits of different forms of transportation and have some knowledge of the location of major airports, ferry ports and motorways.

Certain facilities, such as airports can be used to demonstrate the complexity of the travel and tourism industry. Where possible, visits Will enable candidates to gain an understanding of how various travel and tourism organisations have to work together in order to provide goods and services for travellers and tourists.

Issues relating to tourism management and sustainability at the destinations need to be examined. As with jobs within the leisure industry, there is a wide range of jobs available within the travel and tourism industry. Candidates should be aware of the range of jobs available and the skills and personal qualities required. Candidates would also be hearing first hand about jobs in the travel, tourism and leisure industries from people currently employed in the industry.Centres will need to consider how best to prepare candidates effectively for the examination and to allow sufficient time for revision and examination technique to be developed. Many textbooks have good general material on the leisure and tourism industries, some with case studies of particular organisations.

Several leisure and tourism organisations, particularly tourist attractions, produce information packs that provide general information for students or support material for visits. The Internet has an ever-expanding range of material for use on the courses. Of particular use are the websites set up by the tourist boards and some local Tourist Information Centres, as well as specific visitor attractions. Typically these sites are aimed at those visiting the area and have on-line guides to transport links, leisure and tourism facilities in the area, accommodation and local events.

Marketing Leisure Tourism

Marketing is an important aspect of today's leisure and tourism industries. Whatever the type of leisure or tourism organisation and its motives for providing products and services, the basic principle underpinning marketing is the same: getting the right product to the right people in the right place at the right price using the right promotion.

As the leisure and tourism industries are highly competitive and customers are becoming more demanding, any organisation that does not use marketing effectively will not succeed. There are four key marketing tools that organisations use:

— target marketing;

— market research;

— the marketing mix;

— SWOT analysis.

The marketing activities of leisure and tourism organisations. In detail the marketing activities of one organisation, and produce an item of promotional material for it. Whatever the type of leisure or tourism organisation and its motives for providing products and services, the basic principle underpinning marketing is the same: getting the right product to the right people in the right place at the right price using the right promotion.

It is important for organisations to recognise that different groups of customers, known as 'market segments', have different needs. Target marketing is a tool that helps an organisation ensure that it is offering the right goods and services to the different groups. That markets can be segmented in a number of ways, including by:

— age;

— gender;

— social group;

— lifestyle;

— ethnicity.

Market research is a tool that helps organisations to find out their customers' needs. Market research methods include:

— postal surveys;

— telephone questionnaires;

— personal surveys;

— observation;

— internet.

The different leisure and tourism organisations carry out market research. The term 'marketing mix' is used to describe the key elements that organisation offers in order to meet its customers' needs. It is one of the most important concepts in leisure and tourism marketing. The marketing mix is often referred to as the '4Ps'. These are:

— product;

— price;

— place;

— promotion (how organisations get people to buy their goods and services).

You will need to understand the importance of each of these. This is the term used to describe the product or service that an organisation provides to its customers. It includes:

— the product or service features;

— the brand name;

— the after-sales service;

— product life cycle.

This is the term used to describe what a customer pays for a product or service, including:

— the actual selling price;

— any credit terms;

— profitability

This the term tha^t^ describes how the produce or service reaches the customer, including:

— the types of outlet or facility used;

— the location of outlets or facilities;

— identification of distribution channels.

This is the term used to describe all the methods an organisation uses to tell customers about, and to persuade them to buy its products and services. The different promotional techniques that leisure and tourism organisations use, including:

— advertising;

— direct marketing;

— public relations;

— personal selling;

— displays;

— sponsorship;

— demonstrations;

— sales promotions.

The type of technique which is most appropriate will depend on the type of organisation, the nature of the product or service being promoted, and the type of customer being targeted. For example, a community sports centre would find it more appropriate to advertise in the local paper than on television. Promotional materials include:

— advertisements;

— brochures and leaflets;

— merchandising materials;

— videos;

— press releases;

— internet sites.

The effectiveness of these materials depends on many factors, including the way they are designed, the words and images they contain, and how they are made available to customers.

Leisure and tourism organisations place their own particular emphasis on different components of the marketing mix. Opportunities and threats are outside the control of the organisation. Leisure and tourism organisations need to plan their promotional efforts carefully in order to achieve maximum effect and to make the best use of their resources. They need to consider:

— what a promotional campaign is trying to achieve (its objectives);

— who the target market is;

— what promotional technique(s) to use;

— what promotional materials to use;

— how to monitor and evaluate the success of the campaign.

Candidates are required to complete a portfolio that covers the assessment requirements. To fulfil these requirements candidates need to take part in a planned learning programme covering the knowledge and skills.

Centres should ensure that sufficient time is given to the teaching of the key terms and concepts contained within the unit before embarking on the portfolio. Centres would be advised to approach this unit from the view that the majority of leisure and tourism organisations are businesses and that these organisations have to continually work to provide the right products and services to their customers at the right price using the most appropriate promotional techniques.

The basic principles of marketing are thoroughly understood by candidates at an early stage. It would be good practice to introduce candidates to a range of leisure and tourism organisations to demonstrate the wide range of promotional materials and techniques that are used. These industries produce a volume of material; brochures, leaflets, flyers, TV adverts and this material can be used to exemplify the marketing activities of the tourism industry.

The majority of TV travel programmes, which invariably report on resorts and destinations in a favourable light, should also be seen as marketing tools. Where resources allow visits should be made to leisure and tourism organisations in the locality to allow students to investigate marketing activities. If possible, presentation from marketing managers and other employees will increase the understanding of the candidates and enhance the vocational nature of the course.

Some marketing information is confidential and centres will need to exercise discretion when asking for information. It would be good practice not only to focus on local organisations but also to study the marketing activities of organisations studied, the focus of the early part of the delivery of the unit should be to help candidates to understand what marketing entails.

Some organisations may target new customers as opposed to existing customers, many organisations will differentiate between members and non-members and others may target by geographic area. Also, candidates should appreciate that organisations may not only segment their market by individuals but by groups e.g. a health club might target local businesses to consider corporate membership, a theme park might target coach operators to encourage them to organise visits to the park.

It would be good practice to undertake studies of a range of leisure and tourism organisations within the locality to investigate the various ways in which the markets have been segmented. It is also important to stress the need for market segmentation and to help students understand that for all organisations there will be a finite marketing budget and that it is important that resources are used beneficially. Again the business perspective should be stressed.

Market research can be extremely sophisticated and centres need to consider carefully how to present the concept to candidates. Market research involves the collection, analysis and evaluation of information and data about customers. This information helps leisure and tourism organisations to make decisions about the types of product their customers want and the price they are willing to pay.

Smaller leisure and tourism organisations may only undertake limited market research through a lack of resources or other factors. Before choosing to study organisations as case studies centres should ensure that they will be able to provide appropriate information. If possible, examples of research material should be collected from organisations to illustrate to candidates how the process works.

Although many private sector organisations are unlikely to provide detailed information, public and voluntary organisations may be more forthcoming. It would be good practice for candidates to take part in some form of market research perhaps involving the development of a questionnaire. This would not necessarily involve a visit to the organisation used and could be undertaken outside of the classroom.

Candidates should consider aspects of questionnaire design employed to obtain the required information. Centres should focus on each of the aspects of the marketing mix in turn. Product, price and place should be applied to a range of organisations and factors that affect the components of the marketing mix, other than those listed in the unit should be considered. Centres should ensure that candidates become familiar with terms such as brand name and product life cycle.

Additional time should be allocated to the examination of promotion and it is important that candidates gain an understanding of what the term entails. In particular candidates need to be aware of the significant differences between promotional techniques and promotional materials. Each promotional technique is listed in the unit and should be exemplified using suitable examples from different components of the leisure and tourism industry.

Centres should ensure that candidates have a clear understanding of each technique and why different types of organisation will choose to use different techniques. Similarly, candidates should be exposed to a wide range of promotional materials and be able to identify why different materials are used by different types of organisation.

Some time should be allocated to the study of the effectiveness of promotional materials. If resources allow it would be good practice to study the range of promotional materials used by a particular organisation in conjunction with a visit and have an input from a member of the marketing department to explain why certain materials were successful.

It should be remembered that many leisure and tourism organisations use specialist design companies in the production of promotional materials working to a brief provided by the organisation concerned. The SWOT analysis can be taught through being applied to contrasting leisure and tourism organisations, possibly involving a visit with an input from a member of staff.

Centres should give careful consideration to the use they make of leisure and tourism organisations in the locality. It would be good practice to evaluate what materials and information can be obtained from the organisation before using it as a case study. National organisations can also be used where appropriate.

Candidates will need to study two organisations. One of these organisations must be studied in detail and the contrasting organisation used for comparison as appropriate. There is no reason why all the candidates in a centre cannot study the same organisation.

Portfolio assessment could be partly carried out through student presentations and/or a display, however a report is also expected. When marking student portfolio evidence the following general qualities that distinguish between the levels should be considered:

— increasing depth and breadth of understanding;

— increasing coherence, comparison and drawing of valid conclusions;

— increasing evaluation and analysis;

— increasing independence and originality.

Customer Service

Leisure and tourism organisations depend on customers to buy and use their goods and services. Without customers, businesses cannot succeed. Giving excellent customer service plays an important part in helping organisations keep their customers and attract new ones. Why customer service is so important in leisure and tourism. Because,

— the different needs of customers and how they are met;

— the importance of personal presentation when dealing with customers;

— responding to dissatisfied customers;

— why it is important to keep customer records.

The skills and techniques needed for giving customer service. All leisure and tourism facilities need to make sure their customers are happy with the service they receive because customers are the most important part of any successful business. Customer service includes all contact with the customer, either face-to-face, for example, when selling the organisation's products or services or indirect contact, for example, when dealing with letters of complaint.

Good customer service means putting the needs of the customer first. In organisations that stress good customer service this should be a main aim of all staff. Good customer service requires you, as a member of staff, to put yourself in the position of your customers.

The leisure and tourism organisations recognise the importance of good customer service to the successful selling of their products. Many organisations aim to exceed customer expectations in order to ensure that customers enjoy themselves, leave having enjoyed themselves and return in the future.

Many leisure and tourism organisations ensure that all staff are provided with training in customer service. Customer service training programmes and NVQs are used by many leisure and tourism organisations. There are many different situations in which customer service is provided, for example:

— providing information;

— giving advice;

— receiving and passing on messages;

— keeping records;

— providing assistance;

— dealing with problems;

— dealing with dissatisfied customers;

— offering extra services.

Leisure and tourism facilities are used by a wide variety of people, including those with specific needs, such as disabled visitors and people with young children. All require a high level of customer service. The nature of the provision of customer service will vary between the various components of the leisure and tourism industry.

To provide excellent customer service, you will need to identify and meet the differing needs of a wide variety of customers, including:

— individuals;

— groups;

— people of different ages;

— people from different cultures;

— non-English speakers;

— people with specific needs, for example sight and hearing impaired people, wheelchair access, facilities for young children;

— business men and women.

The customer service includes providing service to both external customers and internal customers. External customers are an organisation's consumers or visitors.

They often pay for products or services and expect to be treated well. External customers are the most important part of a leisure and tourism business; without customers, there would be no business! They must be given the highest standards of service so that they come back again and tell their friends about the good time they had.

The excellent customer service brings number of benefits for leisure and tourism organisations, such as:

— increased sales;

— satisfied customers;

— more customers through repeat business and recommendations;

— a better public image;

— an edge over the competition.

It is also very important that all members of staff give a high level of service to each other. Benefits to the staff and the organisation include:

— a more pleasant place to work;

— a happier and more efficient workforce;

— improved job satisfaction;

— improved chances of promotion within the organisation.

Most people working in leisure and tourism will, at some time, have contact with customers. This may be face to face, over the telephone or in writing. All customers will expect to receive a very high standard of customer service. There are a variety of jobs in leisure and tourism that involve telephone conversations with a range of customers. When communicating with customers you will need to use appropriate:

— language;

— pitch and tone of voice;

— pauses and silences;

— body language.

Most of the time, dealing with customers is a rewarding and interesting experience. From time to time, however, you may have to deal with customer complaints. These could be in writing, over the telephone or face to face.

Many leisure and tourism businesses keep records of their customers. Creating and using up-to-date customer records gives an organisation a clear picture of its business and helps it to plan for the future. For example, a health club might have records of its members' names, addresses, telephone numbers, personal fitness plans and medical details. Accurate records are an essential part of good customer service.

Centres should ensure that sufficient time is given to the teaching of the key terms and concepts within the unit before embarking on the portfolio. However, it is also important to appreciate that many leisure and tourism organisations operate as businesses and the provision of good levels of customer service is one way in which a business can become more profitable and be more likely to succeed.

Throughout the delivery of the unit candidates should be encouraged to view customer service from the perspective of the organisation and should not merely focus on their experiences as customers. The customer is not always right and there are situations where the provision of customer service can present difficult problems for staff, e.g. air rage and abusive customers.

Some centres have used a work experience placement to allow candidates to collect a proportion of the evidence required for the portfolio. This should be seen as good practice providing the placement is within a leisure and tourism context and that centres are aware that candidates cannot guarantee to obtain all of the required information during the course of the placement.

Centres should ensure that candidates are aware of all of the aspects of customer service and, as indicated above, how customer service is vital to the profitability and reputation of the business. Adequate time should be given to discussing the range of situations in which customer service is provided.

Situations in which customer service involves providing information or giving advice imply that the employee has sufficient knowledge about the products and services offered by the organisation. E.g. a hotel receptionist must have a detailed knowledge of all of the departments within the hotel.

The relationship between good product knowledge and customer service should be emphasised to candidates. It would be good practice to develop role-play situations where candidates were able to demonstrate their product knowledge in customer service situations. Other customer service situations may involve providing assistance or dealing with problems. This could be extended to include emergency situations.

All leisure and tourism organisations will have strategies and procedures for emergency situations e.g. fire evacuation procedures, dealing with lost children. Centres should ensure that candidates are aware of the health, safety and security issues relating to customer service and may wish to exemplify how these relate to a range of leisure and tourism organisations.

Centres should ensure that candidates appreciate that leisure and tourism organisations have a wide variety of customers and that staff need to be trained to anticipate the different needs of customer groups. Each of the groups listed in the unit should be discussed and a range of leisure and tourism organisations could be studied to identify their different customer groups.

For certain leisure and tourism organisations customers include other organisations e.g. coach operators are customers of hotels and attractions, airlines are customers of airports. Candidates should be made aware that many organisations have internal and external customers and that the attitudes of staff towards one another within an organisation are important.

It will be difficult to identify the internal customers of small organisations and so larger organisations should be used as case studies. The benefits of customer service should be considered throughout the delivery of the unit.

For private sector organisations good customer service is not only important for its own sake but because it results in increased sales, repeat business, a better public image and in some cases higher profitability.

Centres should provide candidates with a range of opportunities to develop and practice their skills in communicating with customers. Where resources allow, visits can be made to leisure and tourism organisations to allow candidates to study how employees communicate with customers face to face.

Opportunities can also be created where candidates have the opportunity to view other forms of customer communication in operation, such as a call centre. Candidates can be given the opportunity to practice these skills through role-play exercises.

Appropriate attention should be given to the various aspects of communicating with customers listed in the unit and candidates should be made fully aware of the importance of each aspect. Where resources allow candidates should be given the opportunity to observe good customer service being delivered e.g. in a hotel, or being given a presentation by a trained guide or similar person. The information relating to personal presentation should be discussed with candidates.

Many leisure and tourism organisations expect staff to wear a uniform or follow a dress code. The importance of this should be stressed and examples where uniform is worn can be discussed e.g. air cabin crew, fast-food outlets and holiday camp staff. Equally important are discussions about personality, attitude and behaviour. It is far easier to demonstrate poor customer service than to show how it should be done.

There are a number of 'fly on the wall' television programmes showing staff in leisure and tourism organisations dealing with customers in a variety of situations. These could be used to demonstrate how the attitude and behaviour of staff affect the situation, as well as the attitude of the customer. Handling complaints is an undervalued aspect of customer service.

Organisations accept that in a number of cases a customer's complaint may be justified and the organisation will be keen to ensure that the customer is satisfied that the complaint has been dealt with appropriately and will return to the organisation. Organisations are aware that customers may, in extreme cases, take legal action against them if their complaint is not dealt with adequately and larger organisations have sophisticated complaint procedures.

Candidates should be aware that as well as the procedures listed in the unit, there will be situations where a different course of action is required. Role-plays of different situations can be used and if possible, candidates could receive inputs from staff working in customer complaint departments about the nature of the complaints they receive and the procedures employed in dealing with them.

Leisure and tourism organisations keep customer records for a number of reasons. The example given in the unit is of a health club. Candidates should be encouraged to discuss the importance of accurate customer records for this type of organisation. Other types of organisation will have a different relationship with their customers and may use records for marketing purposes.

Candidates should be provided with examples of different formats of customer records used by contrasting organisations. Increasingly these records will be stored electronically. In delivering the unit it would be good practice to use case studies of as many different leisure and tourism organisations as possible.

Candidates should appreciate that the delivery of customer service varies with the nature of the product or service being offered but that staff should always have a positive attitude and try their best to meet the needs of their customers. It would be good practice to approach the assessment of the unit in two sections; one dealing with the customer service provided by a selected leisure or tourism organisation covering the first two strands and the other dealing with the practical delivery of customer service that is covered by the second pair of strands.

Centres will need to ensure that the leisure or tourism organisation selected is able to supply the information and facilities necessary to allow the candidate to fulfil the requirements of the portfolio. The selected organisation will need to have both external and internal customers. Also, it will be necessary for centres to obtain some examples of documentation used by the organisation for dealing with complaints and keeping customer records.

When marking student portfolio evidence the following general qualities that distinguish between the levels should be considered:

— Increasing depth and breadth of understanding;

— Increasing coherence, comparison and drawing of valid conclusions;

— Increasing evaluation and analysis;

— Increasing independence and originality.

Employability in Leisure Tourism

The publication in 1997 of the Dearing Report, 'Higher Education in the Learning Society', heightened the debate on graduate employability. The report provided a vision of higher education for the next twenty years. Key elements of this vision were that participation in higher education should be widened and that investment in learning should contribute explicitly to the development of our society, culture and economy.

It was proposed that fulfilment of this latter objective is partly reliant upon greater consideration being given to the development of students' employability. The report contained specific recommendations relating to employability, including recommendations that; All institutions should, over the medium term, identify opportunities to increase the extent to which programmes help students become familiar with work, and help them to reflect on such experience with immediate effect, works with representative employer and professional organisations to encourage employers to offer more work experience opportunities for students Institutions of higher education begin immediately to develop, for each programme they offer, a 'programme specification' which identifies potential stopping-off points and gives the intended outcomes of the programmes in terms of:

— key skills:

— communication,

— numeracy,

— the use of information technology and

— learning how to learn.

A key element of the Government's response to Dearing was to support recommendations relating to the enhancement of graduate employability. In particular, emphasis was placed upon the need to encourage lifelong learning, the perceived benefits of work-based learning, the need for programme specifications, and the role of 'Graduate Apprenticeships' as a means of bridging the gap between education and employment.

The practical response from the Government has been to pass responsibility to the QAA for ensuring that educational institutions place emphasis on graduate employability. The QAA has published Codes of Practice and benchmark statements that will influence HEIs approaches in this area.

For example, Codes of Practice have been published on Career Education and Placement Learning. These Codes define the expectations against which educational institutions will be reviewed in the future. It is clear that pressure to emphasise employability is also coming from other, non-governmental sources.

For example, at a time when total numbers of applications to hospitality management degree programmes have been falling, there is much competition between academic schools to attract sufficient numbers of applications from suitably qualified prospective students. First destination employment statistics, as an indicator of graduate employability, are often used to gauge the supposed relative quality of hospitality management degree programmes.

In addition, within the hospitality management academic community in recent years there has been a self-generated preoccupation with graduate employability. In academic journals, numerous articles have appeared that dwell upon the characteristics required of graduates if they are to follow successful careers in industry. Interestingly, fewer articles have been written by hospitality management academics about how tutors might facilitate the development of these characteristics.

The apparent link between these subject areas and certain industries (particularly within the field of hospitality) surely generates an assumption that graduates should be equipped with specific knowledge and skills that prepare them for their careers. The challenge for those in higher education is to optimise opportunities for graduates through ensuring the vocational relevance of educational programmes and through developing appropriate industrial contacts.

We must also involve students in learning activities that encourage them to develop skills that are relevant to employers. Crucially, however, we must not let our concern for employability adversely affect the academic credibility of our provision. Ensuring academic credibility should enable universities to attract high calibre applicants for hospitality management degree programmes.

For a variety of reasons, maintaining a public perception of academic credibility within hospitality management education is particularly challenging. In part, this stems from the public association of hospitality employment with operational skills.

There are probably few hospitality management students who have not faced derogatory comments about their studies relating to coffee making or pouring wine. There is an apparent widespread inability to realise that degree-level qualifications are appropriate for those who will be required to manage complex hospitality organisations.

Secondly, in recent years the media have not missed opportunities to report criticisms of vocationally oriented degrees, or to deliberately misinterpret the nature of some degree programmes.

It is also true that the image of hospitality degree programmes suffers precisely because this is a relatively new subject area. Higher education in this field grew out of the activities of professional bodies, but although helping to ensure the vocational content of degree programmes, this has probably not helped to enhance their academic credibility.

In our quest to enhance the employability of graduates it would be naive to distinguish between academic credibility and vocational relevance. We must try to overcome the popular perception that the two are mutually exclusive. It is precisely through their involvement in academic activities that students gain the knowledge and skills that prepare them for successful careers.

The fact that they have specific knowledge of one particular industry should not imply that their education lacked either breadth or depth. The QAA has now published 22 subject benchmark statements, including one for hospitality, leisure, sport and tourism. These statements are designed to provide an outline of the common academic characteristics of UK degrees within each subject area.

In addition, the hospitality, leisure, sport and tourism benchmark statement includes those 'key skills' that all programmes of study should encourage students to develop. An LTSN Internet conference on the subject of benchmarking revealed opposing views about the likely impact of benchmarks.

Whilst some felt that they represent a constraining influence, others championed the transparency that they provide relating to course content. A potentially appealing aspect of benchmark statements for employers is that they provide a clear indication of the skills that graduates are likely to possess, but the arrival of benchmarks has contributed to the controversy surrounding vocational / academic balance, precisely because they are clearly vocationally oriented.

Whilst benchmark statements are generic to all courses within broad subject areas, programme specifications relate to individual programmes of study. The QAA now requires the development of programme specifications that outline the key skills, cognitive skills, and subject specific knowledge that each course will encourage students to develop.

Once again, despite fears about their potential constraining influence, many believe that explicit statements of this nature actually enhance graduate employability. Possibly the most obvious example of our emerging preoccupation with graduate employability is the emphasis that is now being placed on key skills.

Much professional energy has been spent on considering which key skills we should be encouraging students to develop, how best we might facilitate that development and how to assess student performance. LTSN regional seminars have revealed that there are a series of unresolved issues relating to these skills. Specifically, tutors expressed concern about lack of industry feedback regarding which skills are deemed to be appropriate, the difficulty of assessing transferable skills given their intangible nature, and problems with developing skills when dealing with mixed ability groups.

Within vocational higher education there appears to be almost universal agreement that work-based learning can make an important contribution to students' development. In addition, prospective employers often cite appropriate work experience as a vital component of person specifications.

However, it was clear from LTSN regional seminars that significant differences exist in the approaches taken towards the organisation of work-based learning by different educational institutions. In addition, it became evident that whilst some academic departments experience no difficulty in securing the involvement of employers in work experience schemes, for others this is a major obstacle to facilitating this type of learning.

The approach taken towards providing support by personal tutors is seen as having an effect upon graduate employability. A number of academic schools are now adopting a proactive approach that involves scheduled meetings between tutors and their tutees. These meetings provide an opportunity for students to formally reflect upon their performance, consider areas where their knowledge or skills are lacking, and develop strategies to enhance their performance.

This system enables students to record evidence of their skill development in 'progress files' that, it is suggested, enhances their appeal to employers. This contrasts with a more traditional role for personal tutors in which they adopt an 'open door' policy and are there to respond to students who are experiencing difficulties.

LTSN Hospitality, Leisure, Sport and Tourism welcomes the opportunity to disseminate examples of good practice in preparing programme specifications, facilitating the development of key skills and the assessment of these skills, harnessing the potential of work-based learning, and any other issues relating to students' employability.

Gina Ennis-Reynolds, LTSN Liaison Officer for Leisure "The massive growth in the business of leisure education throughout the United Kingdom has continued without necessarily any cognisance of what is required within the leisure industry... In 1996 in England and Wales over 5,000 undergraduates were studying sport, leisure and related areas.

The last decade saw an increasing emphasis on skills development as integral to student's learning in higher education. Most higher education institutions (HEIs) place a great emphasis on key, core and transferable skills in their respective Learning and Teaching strategies.

This move towards an 'employability agenda' has created a tension between those who believe that the purpose of higher education is to encourage students to be independent thinkers, and those who argue that they should be preparing students for employment. Reports and surveys show that employers are able to articulate clearly, their expectations of graduates. The top ten requirements valued by employers according to surveys are:

1) Willingness to learn
2) Commitment
3) Dependability/reliability
4) Self motivation
5) Teamwork
6) Communication skills (oral)
7) Co-operation
8) Communication
9) Drive/energy
10) Self management.

Of these skills, employers find the most significant shortcomings in graduates' oral and written communication skills but are also not very satisfied with their graduate recruits' commercial awareness and financial knowledge, their knowledge of political and social issues and general knowledge, their negotiating skills and their prior knowledge of the job and the organisation.

In terms of specific knowledge, employers are always likely to feel that graduates are less than fully prepared for a specific job. This is only natural - employers want to take on people who can fit into a role with the minimum of training and induction - they will clearly expect this more from graduates than those with lesser academic qualifications.

Whilst personal characteristics such as willingness to learn, commitment, reliability and self-motivation can be encouraged by higher education, they are ultimately individual attributes that are difficult to teach and to assess.

A recent conference on leisure education and employment, run by Manchester Metropolitan University and supported by ILAM sought to address the relevance of academic courses to the leisure industry and whether the proliferation in leisure courses reflected the increasing range of employment opportunities in the sector. This theme has been developed further in a series of seminars and a conference supported by the LTSN.

The MMU conference heard from employers in the public and private sectors with very contrasting experiences of recruiting graduates. Whilst the set of generic attributes above is readily identifiable by employers, it may well be unreasonable to expect specific leisure sector employers to express a consensus view of the bundle of leisure skills and leisure knowledge that they require from potential employees, whether at graduate or any other level.

For example, the requirements of a small, specialist business starting up in the leisure manufacturing sector may be very different from those of a multi-national leisure conglomerate. This potential lack of an explicit 'shopping list' makes it difficult for institutions to respond in a direct and meaningful way. This is largely supported by research in the area.

For example the ILAM guide to careers in leisure used "fifty leading leisure professionals with broad experience in recruiting staff to advise on the basic skills required." This assessment was then used in the form of a 'skills barometer' to show the relative importance of skills for a range of 29 leisure career paths.

The skills were: literacy, numeracy, technical competence, management skills, social and interpersonal skills, marketing skills, any other preferred skills (such as planning skills, political awareness, fundraising skills etc.). However, whilst these skills are drawn from across a range of leisure employment (and not that just requiring a degree qualification) they cannot by any stretch be identified as specific 'leisure skills'. The point here is whether:

(a) it is possible to identify a combination of leisure specific skills and knowledge separate from generic intellectual skills, competencies and personal attributes that leisure sector employees require; and

(b) whether it is appropriate that they are delivered by HEIs as part of courses or by the leisure industry itself as part of induction training. If it is not possible to distinguish specific leisure skills and the majority of employers, whatever their sector, are looking for graduates who are competent in a broad range of general skills, then we have to ask how important is the subject discipline of a degree course to employers?

It may be that a leisure-related degree can add more particular context and knowledge of leisure issues such as commercial awareness, financial knowledge and political and social issues as they relate to leisure. Beyond this, prior knowledge of the nature of a leisure sector job and the organisation in which a graduate may find employment are best provided by either HEIs careers education services or perhaps by the employers themselves.

For those who argue that the purpose of higher education is not to specifically train students for specific careers then the debate about the relevance of particular degree courses is an artificial one. This is supported especially at the undergraduate level by evidence of student motivation in their choice of course.

Most students choose courses based on intrinsic subject interest rather than employment relevance. Surveys on recent graduates report that they would choose their academic programme again if they were returning to university, even if it did not have clear employment relevance. It is relatively easy to imagine students making a decision based less on whether a leisure degree would prepare them well for employment in the leisure sector and more on whether they find leisure interesting as a subject to study for three or more years.

However, the changing nature of funding students in higher education and the increasing levels of student debt may alter this perspective. In any case it does not affect the need to ensure leisure degree courses address the development of core generic skills and knowledge that are relevant to the leisure industry as well as other sectors.

Nor does it affect the need to address the identified skills gap in terms of commercial awareness, financial knowledge and political and social issues as they relate to leisure. In addressing the perceived skills gap between what employers need and what HEIs are producing, a number of models are clear. First is the addition of separate skills development modules or units at the undergraduate level where transferable skills such as team-working, communication, time-management and other 'process-orientated' skills can be taught, developed and assessed.

The second model has been to embed skills within the range of knowledge discipline modules taught for a subject degree course. By doing this it is hoped to make the skills development more meaningful to students. The limited evidence appears to be that: even where key skills are assessed they usually only form a small part of the overall assessment; undergraduate students tend to give a low priority towards modules of skills development compared with discipline modules, that is they are more concerned with content and knowledge rather than process skills; and, the dominant consideration for the student is class of degree rather than the overall development of their skills and knowledge.

HEIs have always been changing and adapting, no more so than now. Setting aside the big issue over the traditional academic role of HEIs and the new emphasis on producing graduates who are more employable - the change in student funding and the need to gain employment to pay off large debts are likely to raise the importance of vocationalism to students in their choice of degree.

In particular, the adapted, opportunist nature of higher education provision in this field, and the youth and fluidity of the sectors that these providers purport to serve, present difficulties for those attempting to identify leisure-specific knowledge and skills. Examination of the historical development of leisure management degrees demonstrates that such programmes have evolved from the diversification and adaptation of a range of disciplines and sub-disciplines.

In some institutions, the re-packaging of physical education and recreation studies or management has led to the development of leisure management, whilst in others the role of diversifying geographers or planners or sociologists has been more influential. In many cases, the presence of a business or management school has been significant in securing a legitimate academic base for the field, and it is possible to identify distinctive approaches in curricula design that can be explained by the historical development of the field at the institutions in question.

However, despite these variations, the majority of leisure management programmes appear to share one particular characteristic in the sense that they are all adaptations of other specialisms, and few - if any - are the outcome of any synoptic view of the exercise in question. Rather, programmes are designed around a conception of vocational preparation emphasising pre-supposed employer requirements, which manifest themselves in the form of conventional management theory.

In some programmes this theory is adapted specifically to leisure or the 'leisure environment', but herein lies a further problem. Academics use a variety of conceptions of leisure when attempting to justify the value of their field to different stakeholders. In validation documents, for example, leisure will often be presented as a time segment determined in relation to work or employment.

Whilst this connects the field to a range of highly important political and economic policy debates, thereby legitimising its position in relation to otherwise sceptical stakeholders, it also enables academics to identify a huge range of careers and corporate bodies as 'vocationally relevant'.

However, in other contexts, academics will use leisure to denote consumption choices made in relation to the activities provided historically by state and local state leisure departments. A range of other, competing conceptions will be employed depending on the occasion and the audience. Thus, a variety of meanings of leisure are being employed in the presentation of exit data, labour market information, placement statistics and throughout the curriculum at different institutions. Identifying craft knowledge, in this context, is clearly problematic.

The field appears to relate either to such a vast range of concerns and occupations that any shared knowledge base is impossible to identify, or to an immature sector in which even the professional associations concerned have struggled to specify a discrete and coherent body of knowledge which simultaneously guides their practice and distinguishes them from other groups.

Leisure management appeals to students because while it carries with it the implied certainty of gainful future employment and the acquisition of appropriate forms of capital, it relies heavily on the notion that leisure is enjoyable, fulfilling and is characterised by intrinsic motivation. In other words, institutions use a further conception of leisure in order to sell the field to prospective students.

Most courses seen to be developed in a piecemeal fashion from lecturer's own interests and without reference to industry mean that the course at Manchester Metropolitan University (developed with Living Well health and fitness company) was considered to represent new practice.

Leisure industry representatives highlighted a wide range of desirable skills and qualities that leisure graduates should possess. These included the so-called 'people management skills' as well as communication, financial, marketing and computing skills. Specific gaps in graduate's abilities seem to include: commercial awareness of the leisure industry and specific technical skills and qualifications.

Bridging the Gap is an Innovations Fund project, which is being financed by the HEFCE. The main aim of the project is to enhance the dissemination of the 1998-2000 round of Innovation Fund projects that have the over-arching theme of graduate employability.

Although few of the projects focused on the hospitality, leisure, sport and tourism subject areas, there were many which may be of interest, including those looking at self-employment, SMEs and students' part-time employment.

In the last ten years, education in Tourism has seen some major changes - it has become an accepted subject for study in Higher Education at many more institutions; and the number and variety of courses on offer has grown to match, and to perhaps exceed, the level of importance placed on the growth of the tourism industry.

In some areas of the UK, tourism is seen as the only reasonable employment alternative where manufacturing industry has almost ceased to exist. Politicians recognise that tourism is a key industry in providing an input into the balance of payments, and that Britain has to compete in a global environment.

Leader of the Liberal Democrats, at a Liberal Democrat one-day conference attended by leaders in the tourism industry on 16 February 2001, said "to remain competitive standards must be raised, greater investment in people and our attractions is vital, and we must market effectively, both at home and abroad.

Certainly the tourism industry has grown in the UK. The value of tourism in 1998 was estimated to be £61.2milllion, and the industry supported 1.7million jobs. It is also estimated that one in five of every new jobs created is a job in the tourism industry. But what jobs are these, and are the courses offered in higher education actually supplying the industry with graduates who have the attributes that employers need in order to achieve the quality required to compete?

Although the value of the industry has grown there is not much evidence to suggest that the structure of the industry has undergone radical alteration - that is the majority of businesses are still SMEs with a much smaller number of big players.

The introduction of benchmarking for tourism courses is welcomed by those who feel there should be some assurance to students and employers that there is a defined basis of knowledge common to tourism courses and despised by others who feel that courses should be able to be differentiated by content and specialisms. John Tribe, in his paper on The National Curriculum for Tourism Higher Education, 1999, suggested, "benchmarking therefore represents the staking out of a compulsory zone within curriculum space".

His thesis proposes a curriculum force field, which illustrates the range of influences on the curricula of tourism degrees, and how they might 'pull' the curriculum in different directions dependent upon the force of the influence exerted. For example there are a range of influences that promote the tourism curriculum as a vocational one for commercial ends, including the needs of employers and professional bodies, but pulling in a different direction are influences that promote the tourism curriculum for non-commercial ends such as host and environmental interests.

If employability of students, and therefore meeting the needs of employers, is going to be seen as a prime influence on what students should be learning within tourism programmes then, under Tribe's model, tourism curricula will be pulled by the influence of employer needs and away from influences for non-vocational and non-commercial ends such as sustainability.

However, it would seem appropriate that both of these influences are taken into account within tourism courses. As Charles Kennedy said " Tourism creates much needed employment in Britain, notably in areas where traditional industries are in decline. But like any activity the benefits of wealth and creation must be balanced against environmental and social consequences."

Employability of students has become a more urgent issue amongst academics as the quality of education offered at institutions is measured against a number of criteria, including how many, and how soon, students get jobs after graduation.

Good scores can mean good publicity and promotional opportunities, ensuring the continuation of courses, an important factor where there is evidence of some universities not being able to recruit sufficient tourism students.

Research at Oxford Brookes University amongst tourism students attending visit days (students who have been offered provisional places) demonstrates that 'getting a good job' on graduation is one of the primary motives for taking the course. At this stage, though, their ideas on what a good job is, and what they need to secure one are vague, and so they rely on evidence of past graduates performance in securing jobs to reassure themselves that they will be able to achieve their aim.

Employers see key and transferable skills as an important element in ensuring that the graduates they employ will be productive in the workplace. Chris Evans of The Tourism Company says that key areas where students must be able to perform are in analytical thought and being able to write.

In most graduate jobs written output will be essential, and students should be able to write well in a number of formats. In the past The Tourism Company has employed graduates who have been well qualified, who have good interpersonal skills and who have interviewed well, only to find that they cannot actually write coherently with appropriate attention to grammar and spelling.

Many other tourism employers endorse this view. A straw poll amongst colleagues who write references for students, showed that when employers contacted referees for further information their primary concern was for students' abilities in key skills. Their academic / intellectual abilities were assumed to be evidenced by their degree qualification, but employers really wanted to know whether graduates could organise their time, work independently, meet deadlines, write letters and make presentations.

Similarly feedback from employers of students on work placement suggests that key skills are the most important elements in making students employable. If they are capable of getting their degrees then they are capable of learning the knowledge they need to be able to do their jobs well, but in order to be quickly useful in the workplace they need competence in the key skills of written communication, but not just reports, working independently, being able to meet deadlines and manage their time, and being able to make presentations suitable for specific audiences.

Students want to be employable in 'good jobs'; employers want graduates with key competencies in addition to subject knowledge; academics want students to be employable as it is one way in which the success of their courses is judged, but also want to take account of other influences on the curriculum; benchmarking provides for core compulsory parts of the curriculum but does not take account of key skills or of the strength of influences on the curriculum at any one time.

Politicians want everything - a good quality sustainable globally competitive industry providing good jobs for people in areas where other industries have declined.

Leisure Tourism Trends: Example of County Borough's

A number of recent government publications providing guidance on tourism, particularly sustainable tourism, emphasize the need for a properly managed tourism industry. Sustainability was prepared as part of a wider government consultation initiative - Opportunities For Change - A Review of the UK Sustainable Development Strategy. This was recently followed by a new strategy document published by the Department of Culture, Media and Sport entitled Tomorrow's tourism: a growth industry for the new Millennium.

For Wales, the Wales Tourist Board have produced a draft successor strategy to Tourism 2000 entitled A New Tourism Strategy For Wales to provide the framework to guide the development of the industry. The strategy confirms that tourism has made excellent progress in achieving ambitious growth targets. Both documents identify the environment and sustainability as the fastest growing themes in tourism. The documents also recognize that environmental goods such as clean water, fresh air and beautiful scenery are fundamental to a range of opportunities that both tourists and the tourist industry have a strong interest in preserving.

South East Wales Authorities are also involved in the preparation of a Regional Tourism Strategy, which will provide a framework for tourism development and marketing initiatives. For the purpose of planning and development plans the guidance on how tourism should be handled is provided in Planning Guidance (Wales) Planning Policy (PGWales) and the associated Technical Advice Note (TAN) 13 - Tourism. DETR Planning Policy Guidance Note 21 on Tourism is also of relevance.

The opportunities for recreation and leisure (of which tourism is a core part) are central components for the functioning of a healthy society. Tourism developments enhance the image of the County Borough, making it attractive to potential industrial developers or those seeking relocation from other areas. Investment in tourism development as well as drawing increased numbers of visitors also provides better recreation and leisure facilities for the residents of the County Borough.

Tourism will provide opportunities for people who are less affluent and those with particular needs e.g. families with young children, the disabled and the elderly. The greater the number of visitors to the County Borough the more important the need for careful management. This must insure that the benefits are not outweighed by damage to the physical environment of the County Borough on which they are based.

The value and volume of tourism and leisure is not totally understood which limits a full analysis of its potential for demand and consequent development. There are a number of reasons for this:-

— The tourism industry does not have a discrete form and no single concept of the industry has been developed and accepted by all industry participants; Within the tourism industry's key activities transportation, accommodation and entertainment, each has developed its own definition, classification and methodologies for data collection.

— The result is that there is little commonly understood or useable communication for tourism. Most attempts at defining tourism have revolved around the definition "what is a tourist". Each industry describes the user differently e.g. as a guest, customer, passenger, visitor, client etc. Because of these problems associated with data collection it is difficult to estimate precisely the value and volume of tourism in Bridgend.

However, Bridgend County Borough Council has adopted the STEAM methodology. It is a computer based analysis package which aims to quantify the value and volume of tourism in the County Borough. It is designed to work at a unitary authority level and above and has provided a more accurate assessment than previous estimates. The assessment for Bridgend for 1998 indicates:-

— Approximately 1,498 full time persons are directly engaged in tourism with another 442 persons indirectly employed;

— Approximately 2,966,000 visitors to the County Borough of which there were 2,407,000 day visitors; 177,000 visitors stayed in serviced accommodation, 181,000 visitors stayed in non-serviced accommodation and 202,000 persons stayed with friends and relatives;

— The overall expenditure by visitors to Bridgend County Borough was about £90 million, of which £18.5 million went on accommodation, £17 million on food and drink, £4 million on recreation, £12 million on shopping and £6.8 million on transport, £22 million was spent indirectly and £10 million on VAT;

— The largest amount of revenue to the area comes from those persons staying in the non-serviced accommodation sector followed by day visitors and finally persons staying in serviced accommodation.

In Porthcawl, which is the main holiday destination in the County Borough the following figures have been established for 1995/96 by research surveys carried out on behalf of the Wales Tourist Board:-

— Tourism related employment is estimated at 19% of all employment;

— 117,000 serviced accommodation bed nights were achieved which equates to 23,400 trips;

— 1.1 million bed nights were achieved in self catering accommodation equating to 137,000 trips;

— 13,000 visitors were visiting friends and relatives (VFR) equating to 6,500 trips;

— One million day trips were made to Porthcawl;

— The total value of the above to Porthcawl was £18.4 million.

The County Borough's tourism potential is high. It has a very attractive coastline and offers a good range of informal outdoor recreation opportunities provided by the Glamorgan Heritage Coast, the Kenfig National Nature Reserve and the Bryngarw Country Park.

The historical and industrial heritage product is strong providing fine examples of Norman castles, former mediaeval farm houses, and Victorian manor houses on the one hand and former ironworks, tram roads and related industrial archaeology on the other. Other activities available in the County Borough include golfing, walking, cycling, surfing and other water sports.

Tourism and Leisure Policies

The following policies will contribute to the key objectives of enhancing, improving and developing the tourist potential of the County Borough whilst protecting and conserving the environment.

Tourism development policy (TM1): New or extended tourist and leisure facilities and attractions will be permitted only where all of the following criteria are satisfied:

1. The development is not located in the countryside, unless it is necessary in the countryside, unless it is necessary in the interests of countryside leisure and recreation;

2. The development will not harm or adversely affect the following areas and their settings;

   a) The glamorgan heritage coast;

   b) The kenfig cSac;

   c) The strategic coalfield Plateau and associated valley sides;

   d) SSSI's and other environmentally sensitive areas;

3. The development will be compatible with, and sympathetic to its surroundings in terms of siting, scale, design, external appearance, materials and landscaping;

4. The development is well located to public transport, the needs of the non car traveller, and the main road network;

5. The highway netweork is capable of accommodating the Traffic Generated by the development without an unacceptable effect on traffic flows and patters, safety, engergy user or other emissions

Opportunities exist for further improving and co-ordinating the range of activities and attractions. The purpose of Policy TM1 is to encourage tourism development which increases the range of activities available to visitors, including support for major crowd drawing attractions in appropriate locations. In the case of Porthcawl there is a recognized need for a critical mass of attractions in order for it to retain and expand its share of the tourist industry.

Proposals for a heritage steam railway line between Tondu and Pontycymmer centred on promoting tourist attractions at various locations along the route is expected to draw a large number of visitors. Such attractions will be expected, wherever possible to be located within, or adjacent to urban areas.

Policy TM1 ensures that proposals for tourist attractions which seek appropriate countryside locations will be related to and in keeping with the surrounding countryside.

As well as the development of specific attractions, Policy TM1 should also relate to the implementation of environmental improvement schemes such as clearance, landscaping, paving, seating, tree planting and building refurbishment particularly in urban areas. This is considered an essential element in further enhancing the attractiveness of the County Borough to visitors.

In this respect the Council is particularly keen to increase the number of visitors to Bridgend town centre and to improve the tourism and leisure provision in and around Bridgend. Tourism/leisure and retailing development at the Designer Outlet Village at Sarn with its shop units, multiplex cinema, themed restaurant and food court has already resulted in increased visitors to the County Borough.

This should now be matched by improvements in the leisure facilities in Bridgend town centre, particularly with the increasing importance of shopping as a leisure and tourism activity. The implementation of pedestrianization, in particular, should see a major improvement in the town centre's environment, as was the case with the pedestrianization of John Street and other environmental improvements in Porthcawl.

Accommodation for visitors in urban areas policy (TM2): The establishment of new serviced and self-catering accommodation, as well as the extension, Upgrading or change of use of building to provide such accommodation, within existing settlements will be favoured provided that all of the following criteria are complied with:

1. The development is compatible with its surroundings in terms of siting scale, design, external appearance and landscaping;
2. Building or areas of historic or architectural interest are not harmed;
3. It will have sufficient car parking within the cartilage of the property;
4. The development is well located to public transport, the needs of the non car traveller and the main road network;
5. The highway network is capable of accommodating the traffic generated by the development without an unacceptable effect on traffic flows and patters, safety, energy use or other emissions

Support and encourage the development of tourist accommodation (TM3): Whilst there is a small number of hotels and guest houses located throughout the County Borough, Porthcawl with its large Trecco Bay Caravan site provides for most of the existing tourism accommodation. In order to increase the attractiveness of the County Borough to both tourists and the business market, an increase in the amount of good quality places to stay is considered vital.

Over recent years great emphasis has been placed on improvements to the range and quality of the self catering and serviced accommodation available, including new hotels and chalet developments. A grants scheme is available from the WTB to encourage hoteliers to raise the standard of their establishments, and to prevent the loss of serviced accommodation to other uses.

In Porthcawl many properties have already benefited from the grant aid scheme which is complemented by the WDA and the County Borough's Town Improvement Grant scheme and by WTB and County Borough's Sense of Place bilingual signage scheme.

The family market accommodation is centred in the Porthcawl area where it is well catered for. There is, however, a deficiency of quality hotels with conference facilities for the business market in the Bridgend area. The relatively large number of firms located in the area form a valuable market for conference and business meetings.

It is important, therefore, that appropriate facilities in terms of meeting rooms, leisure facilities and accommodation of appropriate quality is available. New accommodation projects and improvements in standards/facilities of existing providers specifically catering for the business market will therefore be favourably considered.

Policies TM2 and TM3 are designed to support and encourage the development of appropriately located tourist accommodation (hotels, guest houses and farm houses), particularly in the Bridgend area. Proposals for accommodation in the countryside and designated areas such as the Glamorgan Heritage Coast, the Kenfig National Nature Reserve and other environmentally sensitive areas will be strictly controlled.

Proposals for tourist accommodation are therefore best located within existing settlements. However, the conversion of redundant and disused farm buildings in the countryside can be beneficial. The re-use of old farm buildings, in particular can contribute to, and be in keeping with the character of the countryside.

The re-use of such buildings can often be compatible with the protection of the countryside, but only if the design respects the original features of the building.

Static caravans and chalets policy *(TM4):* New free-standing static caravan chalet for cabin Developments, or the extension of an existing site for such proposes, will not be permitted

Camping and touring caravan sites policy (TM5): Proposal for camping, and touring caravan sites will be permitted only where all of following criteria are satisfied;

1. The development will not harm or adversely affect the following areas their settings:-
   a) The glamorgan heritage coast;
   b) The kenfig cSAC;
   c) The strategic coalfield plateau and associated valley sides;
   d) SSSI's And other environmentally sensitive areas;
2. The development can be Sympathetically assimilated into its surrounding in terms of its siting, scale, design and landscaping;
3. The development is well located to public transport, the needs of the non-car traveller and the main road network;

4. The highway network is capable of accommodating the traffic generated by the development without an unacceptable effect on traffic flows and patters, safety, energy use or other emissions; and
5. The development can be adequatey serviced with water and sewage disposal facilities;
6. The site is not within an area of flood risk.

TAN 13 makes it clear that the development plan needs to ensure that there are sufficient facilities and choice of sites for the touring and static caravaner. New sites should be well screened and will not be permitted in the coastal zone as defined in Policy EV15. Ample provision of caravans exists in Porthcawl and the Coastal Zone which is considered as being a sufficient supply.

Therefore because of the highly intrusive nature of caravan sites the criteria of policy TM5 will be strictly applied. It is however considered that there is room for the provision of further camping and touring caravan sites. These will, however, need to be carefully located and screened so as not to adversely affect the surroundings in which they are situated.

Visitor Attractions Policy (TM6): Proposal for Educational, arts, cultural and entertainment facilities, including restaurants, public houses and cafes will be permitted where:

1. They contribute to the regeneration of town centres by improving their vitality, viabilility and attractivenss to visitors, and enhancing their leisure role in the evening economy and at weekends;
2. The development involves the re-use or adaptation of redudant and disused buildings in urban areas;

3. The proposal does not harm the amenities of people living in the area by means of noise and smells or general usage during unsociable Hours;
4. The development is well located to public transport, the needs of the non-car traveller and the main road network; and
5. The highway network is capable of accommodating the traffic generated by the development without an unacceptable effect on traffic flows and patters, safety, energy use, or other emissions.

There is a recognized deficiency in the provision of arts, cultural and entertainment and leisure facilities particularly in the main towns of the County Borough. This form of development is vital to attracting visitors, as it is linked to improvements in town centre environments and facilities.

Tourism development projects are an integral part of town centre management and regeneration. Policy TM6 provides the impetus for projects which may include the installation of CCTV, decorative lighting, street entertainment and improved signage. Through the implementation of existing strategies the County Borough Council can capitalize on the many opportunities for attracting new visitors and promoting the County Borough as an attractive destination. All tourism development should be based on the principle of equal opportunities.

Porthcawl and the Coastal Zone represent the County Borough's main holiday attraction. Porthcawl should therefore be developed as a major tourist resort by enhancing its tourist potential which will be beneficial to the County Borough as a whole. A regeneration strategy exists for the resort and much has been done to implement its proposals, which has already resulted in major improvements to the physical fabric and infrastructure of the town.

Tourism and leisure attractions in pothcawl policy (TM7): Initiatives and schemes which support the further enhancement and development of prothcawl as the country borough's major tourist resort will be favoured.

Proposals and projects under Policy TM7 for tourism development in Porthcawl will be supported where they contribute to fulfilling the objectives of the regeneration strategy for the resort which are:

— To make the resort of Porthcawl more attractive to visitors and extend the season;

— To raise business confidence and encourage private sector investment;

— To maximize visitor spend and job creation;

— To market the resort effectively to its core family market, whilst developing new markets with growth potential;

— To improve the linkages between the key elements of the resort;

— To strengthen the appeal of the shopping centre and to improve its competitiveness;

— To improve access to the resort.

Key proposals completed to date include the pedestrianization of John Street, the refurbishment of the Grand Pavilion, the refurbishment of the sea front and Esplanade, the construction of a new lifeboat station and the refurbishment of Jennings warehouse. Also the land between the Harbour and Trecco Bay has been allocated under Policy REG3 as a key regeneration site.

Its redevelopment for leisure/entertainment/ commercial/ accommodation purposes will play a crucial role in strengthening the resort's position as a leading tourism attraction.

Protection of existing serviced accommodation Policy (TM8): The purpose of Policy TM8 is to resist the loss of hotel stock to other uses which can seriously weaken a resort's ability to maintain its status as a tourist destination. This is supported by advice contained in TAN13 on tourism. The availability of a wide range of serviced accommodation benefits the economy in general and gives choice to intending visitors.

TAN13, however, advises that the planning system should not be used to perpetuate outdated accommodation for which there is no demand. The County Borough Council therefore accepts that instances may arise where conversion may be justified for one of the reasons stated under Policy TM8.

In assessing applications for conversion to alternative uses, the Authority will take into account the length of time a property has been vacant for on the market, trends in occupancy rates and customer preferences, the suitability of the building in terms of size and floor layout for the provision of modern serviced accommodation.

5

Nature-based Tourism

Tourism can be defined as "the activities of persons travelling to and staying in one place outside their usual environment for not more than one consecutive year for leisure, business and other purposes". It can be seen as an interaction between supply and demand, where a product is developed to meet a need. Sustainable tourism combines conservation principles with tourism development. Sustainable tourism development is about making tourism more compatible with the needs and resources of a destination area. It offers a broader approach to tourism practices and a built-in ability to control the rate and scale of tourism growth -if stakeholder responsibility is successfully exercised.

It is both important and relatively easy to distinguish between two general categories of tourism. They are mainstream tourism and special interest tourism.Mainstream tourism captures the largest market segment of tourism. It consists of people looking for rest, novel experiences and recreation, and often occurs at beaches and in cities. These travellers desire comfortable hotels and the presence of other tourist accommodations, such as a resort complex that offers shopping, recreation, restaurants, entertainment and other facilities and services. This tourism often occurs in high volumes, which is why it is often referred to as mass tourism. Visitors are segmented into different mainstream tourism markets based on characteristics such as nationality, social class, spending power, age and stage of life.

Special interest tourism consists of people who possess a common special interest that influences their travel choices. These visitors are segmented by specific interests or motivations rather than by other characteristics such as age or social class. The type of travel experience that they seek is strongly related to their special interest. Nature tourism, in all its specialised forms, is an example of special interest tourism.

Nature-based Tourism

Nature-based tourism is primarily concerned with the direct enjoyment of some relatively undisturbed phenomenon of nature. The degree to which a visitor's experience depends upon nature can vary. There are activities:

a) which are dependent on nature (e.g., people seeking to observe animals in the wild require a natural environment to enjoy their experience)

b) which are enhanced by nature (e.g., people prefer to camp in a forest but the activity might be possible with equal satisfaction for some users without a purely natural setting)

c) for which the natural setting is incidental (e.g., if a person's interest is a cooling swim then the setting may be relatively unimportant, assuming unpolluted water).

Nature tourism is a sufficiently broad term that it can be applied to a broad range of different landscapes and tourism destinations. It should be stated that although the term nature-based tourism places focus on the natural aspects, it is recognised that the natural environment contains cultural components, and therefore, although not always stated, cultural aspects are included in discussions about nature tourism. Many terms exist that describe different types of nature-based tourism. These terms attempt to differentiate nature travel by more specific factors.

There are many subtle and sometimes ambiguous differences between all of these terms, which make identifying specific and comprehensive definitions for all of these nature-based tourism terms difficult and time consuming. Nature plays a primary role in attracting tourists to specific destinations, so in this sense most tourism may be described as nature-based.

Nature-based tourism can occur as mass tourism to destinations compatible with high volumes of people, such as beach resorts, touring, and cruise vacationing. Nature-based tourism can also occur as special interest tourism with destinations such as nature observation in a forest, fishing in a stream, or canoeing in a lake. A group of nature tourism visitors may all have a more specific common interest, such as enjoying hiking in mountains. These visitors will choose locations where this is available, making it possible to market to them a collection of destinations that meet those criteria.

By adding a motivation component, it is possible to see that the types of visitors who choose special interest tourism are more likely to possess motivations that will support the goals of sustainable nature tourism. Beach tourists may be motivated by relaxation and entertainment. This does not imply any interest in learning about the special natural features of the area, nor any responsibility to ensure that their vacation maximises positive impacts to the environment and surrounding communities while minimising the negative ones.

Nature-based tourists are usually motivated by education and personal enrichment. The motivations of the latter are closely correlated with objectives of a more specific form of special interest nature-based tourism, called ecotourism. .

Ecotourism

A specific type of nature-based tourism is ecotourism. It is nature-based tourism that involves education and interpretation of the natural environment and is managed to be ecologically sustainable. For tourism to be ecologically sustainable, there must be an appropriate return to the local community and a contribution to the long-term conservation of the resource. A distinction exists between nature-based tourism and ecotourism.

Nature-based tourism is a broader term, concerned in general with the enjoyment of nature (which may or may not contribute directly to nature conservation). For a specific nature-based tourism experience to qualify as an ecotourism experience, more specific criteria must be present (than those defined by nature tourism), such as an identifiable contribution to conservation (recall that not all nature tourism automatically contributes positively to conservation efforts). Because the term has different meanings, it is difficult to state exactly all the criteria. Adding to the confusion is the opportunistic and sometimes inaccurate use of the term in marketing. The terminology is sometimes liberally applied to a range of businesses, products and services (even though a large difference can exist in the sustainable efforts made by these companies) because marketers and advertisers know it appeals to the consumer's desire to support environmentally friendly products.

Most ecotourism definitions address some combination of motivation, philosophy, conduct and economic benefit to conservation. Butler identifies ecotourism as: a) an activity, b) a philosophy, and c) a model of how to approach the environment.

Ecotourism is a word with many meanings. Some use it to attract visitors to their business, others use it to define a combination of interests. It encompasses both nature-based and recreational tourism. There are many theories and concepts associated with ecotourism, and its true definition is only understood by those who are aware of these concepts. Hopefully, this confusion will change in the near future.

There are various definitions of ecotourism, most of which have to do with combining the travel industry with an ideal that emphasizes conservation and preservation of the wilderness in which people spend their vacations.

The Ecotourism Society defines ecotourism as "responsible travel which conserves environments and sustains the well-being of local people". Although this is a loosely constructed definition, the truth is that ecotourism has different connotations to different people in their varying relationships within the ecotourism industry, from tour operators to conservationists, to actual tourists.

The World Wildlife Fund, who has a vested interest in the ecotourism industry in terms of wilderness protection for habitats and various species present, believes "the term ecotourism refers to any travel to or through wilderness areas that has minimal impact on the natural environment and its wildlife while providing some economic benefits to local communities and the area's indigenous stewards".

Ecotourism incorporates many different activities that individuals enjoy in nature, usually that are more physically active than the typical vacation to a resort where one is pampered and is determined to relax. Ecotourism tends to incorporate activities such as hiking, camping, observing wildlife in its habitat, mountain climbing, and water sports of different kinds. Water sports will be the focus of this proposal, specifically kayaking, canoeing, and white water rafting.

The typical person who is interested in ecotourism and has taken to participating in these activities are "in their 30s and 40s, with more travelers above that range than below it. Women are as active as men. Most enjoy above-average incomes and educations, and have traveled widely already to more conventional destinations. Now they are looking for something different".

These travelers are in search of something different for this vacation, as they have already experienced the typical vacation. They seek a more active and modern alternative, which is met in ecotourism. Not only is it a physical challenge, in most cases, but it is also a chance to learn respect for nature, and for some, a chance to do some self-reflection, inspired by the beauty of their surroundings.

There are some definite trends that have been occurring over the last thirty years, and especially the last decade, that indicate that ecotourism is becoming an increasingly popular option for travel. Tourism is the world's fastest growing industry, and this includes ecotourism.

Statistics indicate that "tourism grew by nearly 300% between 1970 and 1990, and is expected to grow by half again before the end of the century. In 1991, 450 million international travelers generated more than $3 trillion in tourism revenues. About 15%, or nearly 68 million, of these travelers participated in nature-related trips" . Although not all of these "nature-related" trips constitute ecotourism, it does show an increasing interest for outdoor activities, and possibly, education.

The growth of ecotourism, specifically, is indeed a reality, although, as we stated before, ecotourism has many different definitions. It is estimated by the "World Tourism Organization, based in Madrid, found in one recent study that global spending on ecotourism was increasing by 20% a year-about six times the average rate of growth for the tourism industry.

Although prescriptions and guidelines have emerged to promote successful implementation, standardardized or widely-utilized methods to identify the potential and gauge the progress of ecotourism sites have yet to emerge. In this situation, the availability and application of a framework with which to define and evaluate the functions and status of ecotourism at the site level may assist in understanding gaps between ideal prescriptions and ground-level failure, and encourage and facilitate the achievement of goals for ecotourism at an operational level.

Throughout the 1980's and 1990's, widespread environmental interest fostered trendy "environmental opportunism" and encouraged loose uses of the pre-fix "eco". Promotion of ecotourism, with or without a hyphen, and in the absence of a clear indication of meaning, often resulted in use of the term being little more than a marketing tactic to give businesses an apparent green edge on the competition. However, at the same time, world-wide, a growing expanse of land and sea has come to be exploited to cater to the demands of an expanding number of people seeking nature for pleasure and it has become clear that such tourism ultimately relies on the availability and quality of natural areas and, therefore, must be considered alongside strategies for maintaining and protecting nature. Those at the forefront of ecotourism research and development now provide definitions which address the fundamental goals of conservation of natural areas and local development.

In ecotourism, natural areas and local populations are united in a symbiotic relationship through the introduction of tourism. Ecotourism is viewed as a means of protecting natural areas through the generation of revenues, environmental education and the involvement of local people. In such ways, both conservation and development will be promoted in a sustainable forms (all malleable and contested concepts). Unfortunately, on the ground, distinction between ecotourism and other forms of tourism are often not evident and are widely debated. Discrepancies are a result of the variety of different perspectives and criteria used to distinguish ecotourism. These include the motivations for initiating ecotourism (e.g. as a conservation strategy, a business venture, or as part of an environmental education campaign), the motivations of users, the presence and scale of environmental, social and economic impacts, and the presence and quality of services offered.

Proponents of ecotourism have attempted to overcome such differences by developing valueladen ethical principles as criteria for distinguishing ecotourism. Ecotourism, requires embodiment of "intrinsic rather than extrinsic values" reflecting a "biocentric rather than homocentric philosophy". In addition to ascribing to environmental ethics, tourists themselves are described as "purposeful" and "environmentally responsible" travelers. However, such descriptors do not address the functions of ecotourism and what it is expected to achieve, nor do they lend themselves readily to measurement and evaluation.

In addition to a definition of what ecotourism is, there should be consideration of what is to be achieved through ecotourism. In a symbiotic relationship between local populations and protected area resources or biodiversity, local residents act as stewards of the natural resources and, in return, they benefit from protected areas through sustainable harvesting, integrated and multiple use zones, and protection of important resources such as water catchments. Often, the relationship between local communities and resource use, particularly in the peripheral locations common to many ecotourism sites, is one where dependence on resource exploitation is high and, thus, attempts to regulate or prohibit resource use may be unrealistic and antagonistic to local people. Livelihoods based on activities such as slash and burn agriculture, cattle farming, hunting, fishing, wood collection, timber harvesting and mineral extraction require substantial amounts of natural resources (water, trees, game, minerals and, most of all, land and soil) to sustain large populations. Implementation and enforcement of use restrictions may foster confusion and resentment on the part of local people accustomed to using such lands and resources. In such situations, local people may become opponents of tourism and undermine its operation. Such obstacles to the success of ecotourism can often be countered by involving local people in planning and management processes, whereby they have some control over and agreed-upon access to the resources they require.

Even so, it is quite possible that in some circumstances local people may not welcome tourism at all and that view should be respected, but in many developing countries and in peripheral locations in socalled developed countries, tourism is often seen to be one among a limited number of development options. Relationship indicators are measurable variables which may be used to reflect antagonistic or symbiotic links between people and resources. An evaluation employing such indicators can provides insight into the challenges and possibilities for local development, capacity building, and ecotourism.

The characteristics of communities will influence the extent to which ecotourism affects social changes and attitudes towards tourism and conservation. For example, social and familial cohesion may encourage the spreading of positive attitudes (if an individual benefits, it may be viewed as a benefit to the broader community), in contrast to a community where individuals are only concerned for their own personal benefits. Furthermore, communities already exposed to outside influences, exogenous technological advances or other forms of change, will likely respond differently to development opportunities than populations which have not experienced such changes.

Similarly, characteristics of ecosystems reveal a natural area's capacity to withstand activities such as resource harvesting, which may be required or desired by local communities. In addition to the benefits which may accrue from protection of resources, local residents may receive a variety of benefits from becoming host communities for ecotourists.

By participating in ecotourism, communities can receive tangible economic, infrastructural and social benefits - benefits which are less likely to leak out of the community if participation is local. In turn, experiences of tourists may be enhanced by opportunities to interact with local people. If positive attitudes to ecotourism are to be fostered, residents living in or adjacent to a protected area should be receiving economic and social benefits or compensations which will support or complement their livelihoods.

Local economic benefits from ecotourism have been documented both in the form of increased employment opportunities and incomes, community sharing in the distribution of revenues, and compensations. Thus, the introduction of ecotourism can encourage socio-economic development, if it is desired by the community. External judgments and assumptions about the benefits of development, however conceived, should be avoided.

Whether increased economic activity or changes in the educational system of a rural area are needed or desirable may be a point of dispute. Such a perspective emphasizes again the importance of involving members of destination communities as stakeholders in tourism planning and decision making. The interrelatedness of people-resource-tourism relationships is likely to be evident in the attitudes of local peoples: if local people are already disgruntled about resource-use restrictions from protected area regulations, it is likely that this negativity may influence attitudes towards tourism development.

However, communities should not be encouraged to become solely dependent upon ecotourism: rather, ecotourism ideally should complement other activities and help to diversify an economy. Tourism of any type should not be viewed in isolation and its development should be considered as part of a broader plan for the use of resoucres. The challenges in developing such plans should not be underestimated for reasons as diverse as the fact that powerful interests may benefit from the absence of a plan and governments in some locations have withdrawn from many planning functions in favour of the operation of an unfettered market.

The contributions which ecotourism can make to biodiversity and the integrity of natural areas are as important as the potentially positive affects on adjacent communities. The provision of environmental education through enhancement of opportunities to appreciate nature is fundamental to the success of ecotourism. Biodiversity and natural areas can provide this service in return for economic revenues which can contribute to protected area conservation. Many people who travel to natural areas do so specifically to indulge in experiences with nature, regardless of what activities they choose to do. It is the responsibility of the managers of a protected area to ensure the quality of the available natural experiences and to work towards instilling 'transformative values' (values which, through a learning experience with nature, yield greater environmental awareness, appreciation and respect for nature. Protected areas can be viewed as natural laboratories, living museums, retreats, havens, and outdoor schools, and provide unique, interactive opportunities for promoting environmental stewardship for both locals and visitors.

Education, through passive (in the form of reading materials, maps, signs, information centres) and perhaps active interpretation (such as guided tours, talk groups, theatre), if not too intrusive and depending upon program objectives, are forms of tourist management in themselves. They also can add to the visitors' experiences, direct people towards appropriate behaviours and, again, encourage appreciation of natural areas which can result in environmental advocacy.

Tourism revenues can make a substantial contribution to the costs of managing protected areas. A surplus from tourism revenues (over $560 000/year) at Galapagos National Park, Ecuador, allows some funds to be redistributed to other protected areas in Ecuador. However, the magnitude of revenues depends largely on the type of management objectives sought and the type and amounts of revenues pursued. There are many other factors apart from those at the site-level, which influence the capacity for effective environmental education and revenue-capturing. National and regional policies will dictate the limits of possible contributions from tourism revenues and the quality of support available to implement management strategies. Often it is not possible to earmark revenues which must be remitted to central governments and are not returned to the protected area responsible for their collection.

The development of positive relationships between people, resources and tourism is very unlikely to occur without implementation of effective policies, management strategies, and involvement of a wide range of organizations, including NGOs and, in developing areas, conservation and development assistance agencies. The qualities of protected area policies and of those who are employed to carry them out may influence everything from the extent of resource exploitation which occurs, to the amount of revenue generated and the quality of interpretation. NGOs, research teams and conservation and development-assistance agencies have important roles to play, particularly in rapidly-developing tropical countries where funding for the preparation of management plans or community development programs may be insufficient and personnel with the necessary knowledge, skills and training may be lacking. Such agencies may assist in developing data bases for natural areas and also can provide opportunities for education and local capacity building through the hiring and training of local people.

Ecotourism should be regarded as being more than tourism to natural areas and should be viewed as a means of combining the goals of resource conservation and local development through tourism in a synergistic fashion. This means that care should be taken to ensure that the goals of tourism development do not interfere with the goals of protecting natural areas and biodiversity. Ecotourism should function under the premises that, among other things, natural resources are finite and their appreciation and protection can be fostered through education, and the presence of supplementary sources of income from tourism will encourage residents to become stewards of their environment. Ideally, local populations may become advocates for protection of their natural resources and take pride in the unique surroundings which attract outsiders.

If planning and decision-making do not involve local populations, then ecotourism will not succeed, and may even be detrimental to local communities. Many interrelated processes influence the potential and success of ecotourism within a protected area and links between natural areas, local people and tourism have been highlighted in this matter.

Agritourism

When agricultural direct marketers view their business as a tourist attraction as well as an agricultural enterprise, many new sources of information and opportunity become available. A visitor to a farm or ranch who wants a farm or rural experience as much as to buy agricultural products is a tourist. The number of visitors to farm outlets who are interested in a farm or ranch experience is increasing. Some of the most successful direct marketing operators recognized the potential of selling a farm or ranch experience early.

In a study of agritourism in New York State, 63% of the 17 farm tour enterprises contacted had increased in size between 1986 and 1991. All but one of the remaining enterprises had stayed the same size. Over 3/5ths of all visitors were school children who paid admission for the tour. Admissions for children ranged from \$.50 to \$1.75 while the typical adult admissions were \$2.50 to \$3.50. The biggest problems cited by tour operators were dealing with visitors (especially interruption of farm activities and visitors' treatment of animals), liability insurance, labour and marketing.

Catering to 'agricultural tourists' is especially important at direct farm marketing outlets that are located farther away from urban centers. More distant farm outlets will have to offer more than just products to stay competitive as new farm outlets spring up near major urban areas. One way to stay competitive is to understand what visitors are looking for in a farm experience and to provide services that appeal to visitors. Understanding visitors is an important step towards dealing with them and marketing to them.

A couple of important trends have shown up in recent tourism studies. Aside from growing as an activity, tourism is changing shape. People are taking more short vacations rather than one long vacation each year. There is a growing interest in vacations that involve doing or experiencing. Hence, the growth in the "new" tourisms: ecological, cultural, heritage and agricultural tourism. Finally, there is a steady increase in outdoor recreation by tourists. These trends are due to demographic, economic and cultural changes.

These changes include the aging of the population, the shrinking size of households and the increasing urbanization of the population. Other trends affecting tourism are the increase in the number of two earner households and the increasing interest of the populace in the environment.

Tourism is an activity that involves a large array of retail and service businesses. The sectors most affected by tourism are hotels and other lodging facilities, eating and drinking establishments, and amusement and recreation facilities such as theme parks and ski resorts. One of the largest expenses in these industries is salaries and wages for employees. Often these employees are from the local area. However, for some businesses that are highly seasonal, employees may come from outside. Some communities worry about relying too heavily on tourism.

Some of the negative aspects of tourism may include the highly seasonal nature of employment, the low average wage level in tourism related industries, the congestion and increases in prices of products and real estate that tourists can cause. However, well managed tourism can complement other economic activities in a community.

One positive aspect of tourism is its ability to bring new money into the community. Multipliers in industries that serve tourists are relatively high because wages and salaries are such a large part of the industries' total expenses. The impacts of tourism can be increased by selling local products and by helping local people retain ownership of businesses that serve tourists.

Agricultural tourism is particularly high in impacts because the labour used, business ownership and the products sold are usually local. There are two basic ways for a community or a business to increase revenues from tourism. Either increase the number of visitors or increase the amount that each visitor spends. This is why local chambers of commerce have devoted so much of their resources to attracting more visitors to the area.

In an area that may have limited visitor accommodations, attracting day visitors may be the most effective strategy to pursue. However, in communities that do have hotels and other lodging, convincing visitors to stay overnight is the most effective way to increase visitor expenditures. Not only do such visitors spend additional money on lodging, they eat more meals in the community and have more time to shop in local stores. In most surveys of visitors, shopping is one of the most popular vacation activities.

An effective way for individual businesses to increase their sales to visitors is to offer a range of products and services that will keep the visitor at their outlets longer. Many grocery stores are arranged to slow shoppers down because typically the longer a person is in a store, the more they are likely to spend.

In the study of agricultural tourism in Cochise County, 81,450 non-local visitors spent close to one million dollars and generated $1.9 million in sales impacts in the county. While the average expenditure per visitor party was $58, overnight visitors spent $130 per visitor party. Overnight visitors spent nearly four times as much as day trip visitors. To convince a visitor to make an extended trip to an area, there have to be enough activities or places to visit. In rural communities there may not be enough to do in a single community to keep a visitor in the area for more than a few hours.

If a group of communities work together and promote their whole region, they may be much more successful in both attracting visitors and convincing them to stay more than just for a day. This is why although attracting tourists is a competitive affair, businesses that cooperate with each other in order to attract visitors are more likely to succeed than those businesses that decide to 'go it alone'. Other sections of this manual provide more information about who visitors are and what they want, and on effective means of advertising and promoting 'agricultural tourism'.

Rural Tourism

No internationally accepted definition of rural tourism exists at present. Nevertheless, since tourism is more a demand-side concept, the following basic definition can be used to describe rural tourism:

> Rural tourism is the activities of persons travelling to and staying in rural areas (without mass tourism) other than those of their usual environment for less than one consecutive year for leisure, business and other purposes (excluding the exercise of an activity remunerated from within the place visited).

Since rural tourism involves travelling to and staying in rural areas, one must define the rural tourism area. The proposed definition of tourism rural areas is based on two basic criteria:

— size and density of population

— tourism accommodation supply of each locality.

Rural tourism areas are thinly populated areas supplying limited tourist accommodation capacity. Therefore the study of rural tourism excludes all tourism activities in urban areas and in over-exploited rural tourism areas. The rural visitor is defined according to the definition of the visitor. The term "rural" simply describes the type of destination visited.

Rural tourism is determined solely by the group of internal visitors and by the territories involved. Neither products nor enterprises enter into the definition. Thus, to identify rural tourism both demand and supply must be taken into account. All products purchased by rural visitors or sold by enterprises to rural visitors in the rural area are regarded as part of rural tourism.

Three fundamental types of statistical unit are involved in surveys and analysis of rural tourism:

— the consumer unit: individual or household which is used in demand surveys

— the producer unit: enterprise, establishment which is used in supply surveys or censuses

— the territorial unit.

Since rural tourism is both demand-and supply-oriented, the basic methodology for tourism demand and supply also applies to rural tourism statistics, as a subset of tourism demand and supply-side statistics.

The demand variables and classifications presented in "Overnight visits and same-dats visits" should be used. Special attention should be placed on the destination, purpose and activities undertaken during the visit. The main purpose of the topographical grouping of the destination is to identify classes of territorial units which are homogeneous with regard to their main natural tourism resources. This would allow us to compare the development of similar locations within countries or regions.

Variables on income, age, and the household and travelling party composition may be of importance in determining the destination. The desire to visit rural areas may also depend of the place of residence of the visitor, the topography of his place of residence and housing conditions.

The purpose of the visit should be closely linked to the activities undertaken by the visitor in the rural area, and if possible the frequency of these activities during the visit. As well as the main means of transport used for the visit, the means used in the rural area should be recorded. Likewise, more than one type of accommodation may be used during a visit spent totally or partly in a rural area, so all types used should be recorded according to the number of nights spent per type of accommodation. Information on the organisation of visits may be a useful input in deciding how to promote rural tourism. Finally, concerning expenditure, only the expenditure on goods and services consumed from the rural area should be taken into account.

Rural tourism products are defined as goods and services provided to visitors in rural areas. The goods and services whose production has used resources from the rural area should be presented separately. For certain economic activities and products, it is proposed to distinguish those especially relevant to rural tourism. In principle, all the groups of tourist accommodation may be provided in rural areas. To obtain a fuller picture of "spa" tourism, it is proposed to distinguish the services of hotels and similar establishments which provide health facilities.

The transport services supplied to rural visitors to take them to the rural area are generally not profitable to the rural economy. Therefore, the transport services supplied during the visitor's stay in the rural area are to be presented separately. This means that passenger land and water transport will be the most relevant activities.

Rental services of cars, motorcycles, caravans, and leisure and pleasure equipment supplied in the rural area are all relevant for the rural visitor. Concerning leisure and pleasure services, it is proposed identify those which are of importance for rural tourism, e.g.: bicycles, pleasure boats, rowing boats, canoes and kayaks, winter sports equipment, horses used for riding. Finally many recreational, cultural and sporting products are supplied to visitors in the rural area.

The same variables as presented in "Tourism supply" apply to rural tourism supply. Concerning tourism accommodation, data on the capacity of bed-places per territorial LOC unit should be collected in order to classify administrative territories into rural and non-rural areas. It is useful to analyse the development of the low-capacity groups, especially in relation to rural tourism policy. Other variables which are of specific interest to the analysis of rural tourism relate to general data on turnover for different activity and product groups, value added and employment.

The methodological framework drawn up for rural tourism statistics uses generally accepted classifications for products and activities. This means that links to other general sectoral statistics are possible. The geographical classifications proposed, i.e. the NUTS and LOC, also facilitate comparisons with other statistics at regional level. Rural tourism also holds links with population and environment statistics.

With regard to agricultural statistics, agri-tourism is considered to be part of rural tourism as a whole, and can only be identified from the establishments classified as agricultural holdings within the NACE. Given the criterion of "main activity", only part of the agricultural holdings in the Farm Structure Survey population will be considered as agricultural tourism establishments. Statistics on agri-tourism as such must, therefore, use the farm population as a starting point. Efforts must be made to avoid double counting and the assignment of agri-tourism to other parts of rural tourism.

Data on the demand for rural tourism can be obtained from the survey methods presented in "Overnight visits and same-day visits" If detailed questions are asked about the region visited, the topography of the destination, kind of accommodation used, reasons for the visit and activities performed during the trip, these surveys may be able to describe the general demand pattern for visits to rural areas.

Restrictions placed upon sample size and costs of coding do not normally allow for the detailed geographical breakdown required for a classification of the destination with regard to its "rurality". As a result, detailed information on tourism demand relating to a local area must be obtained through on-the-spot surveys in the form of interviews or questionnaires filled in by the visitor personally. All types of demand surveys are relevant since they may be used to support each other.

6

Sustainable Tourism

Tourism is reputed to be the world's largest economic sector, and one with a vested interest in the environment and the resource base on which it depends. While tourism provides considerable economic benefits for many countries, regions and communities, its rapid expansion can also be responsible for adverse environmental and socio-cultural impacts. Natural resource depletion and environmental degradation associated with tourism activities are sometimes serious problems in tourism-rich regions. The management of natural resources to reverse this trend is thus one of the most difficult challenges for governments at different levels. The fact that most tourists chose to maintain their relatively high patterns of consumption and waste generation when they reach their destinations can be a particularly serious problem for developing countries and regions without the appropriate means for protecting their natural resources and local ecosystems from the pressures of mass tourism.

The main environmental impacts of tourism are: (a) pressure on natural resources, (b)pollution and waste generation and (c) damage to ecosystems. It is now widely recognized that not only uncontrolled tourism expansion is likely to lead to environmental degradation, but also that environmental degradation, in turn, poses a serious threat to tourism. In addition to pressure on the availability and prices of resources consumed by local residents – such as energy, food and basic raw materials – the main natural resources at risk from tourism development are land, freshwater and marine resources.

Without careful land-use planning, for instance, rapid tourism development can intensify competition for land resources with other uses and lead to rising land prices and increased pressure to build on agricultural land. Intensive tourism development can also threaten natural landscapes, notably though deforestation, loss of wetlands and soil erosion.

Tourism development in coastal areas – including hotel, airport and road construction – is a matter for increasing concern worldwide as it can lead to sand mining, beach erosion and land degradation. Freshwater availability for competing agricultural, industrial, household and other uses is rapidly becoming one of the most critical natural resource issues in many countries and regions. Rapid expansion of the tourism industry, which tends to be extremely water-intensive, can exacerbate this problem by placing considerable pressure on scarce water supply in many destinations.

Water scarcity can pose a serious limitation to future tourism development in many low-lying coastal areas and small islands that have limited possibility for surface water use and storage, and whose groundwater may be contaminated by saltwater intrusion. Over-consumption by many tourist facilities – notably large hotel resorts and golf courses – can limit current supplies available to farmers and local populations in water-scarce regions and thus lead to serious shortages and price rises.

In addition, pollution of available freshwater sources, some of which may be associated with tourism-related activities, can exacerbate local shortages. Rapid expansion of coastal and ocean tourism activities, such as snorkelling, scuba diving and sport fishing, can threaten coral reefs and other marine resources.

Disturbance to marine aquatic life can also be caused by the intensive use of thrill craft, such as jet skis, frequent boat tours and boat anchors. Anchor damage is now regarded as one of the most serious threats to coral reefs in the Caribbean Sea, in view of the growing number of both small boats and large cruise ships sailing in the region. Severe damage to coral reefs and other marine resources may, in turn, not only discourage further tourism and threaten the future of local tourist industries, but also damage local fisheries.

Besides the consumption of large amounts of natural and other local resources, the tourism industry also generates considerable waste and pollution. Improper disposal of liquid and solid waste generated by the tourism industry has become a particular problem for many developing countries and regions that lack the capacity to treat these waste materials properly. Disposal of such untreated waste has, in turn, contributed to reducing availability of the above-mentioned resources at the local level.

Apart from the contamination of freshwater from pollution by untreated sewage, tourist activities can also lead to land contamination from solid waste and the contamination of marine waters and coastal areas from pollution generated by hotels and marinas, as well as cruise ships. It is estimated that cruise ships in the Caribbean Sea alone produced more than 70, 000 tons of liquid and solid waste a year during the mid-1990s. The fast growth of the cruise sector in the region may have exacerbated this problem in recent years. Furthermore, a particular cause of concern for coastal areas and small islands is the illegal disposal of sewage, solid waste and cargo residues by merchant ships, which cause marine and beach pollution.

In addition, relatively high levels of energy consumption in hotels – including energy for air-conditioning, heating and cooking – as well as fuel used by tourism-related transportation can also contribute significantly to local air pollution in many host countries and regions. Local air and noise pollution linked to exhaustive tourism development or urban congestion can sometimes even discourage tourists from visiting some destinations.

Intensive tourism activity in natural areas can interfere with fragile vegetation and wildlife and cause irreversible damage to ecosystems, particularly if the infrastructure in those areas is not adequately prepared to absorb mass tourism.

Uncontrolled tourism activities can lead to the severe disruption of wildlife habitats and increased pressure on endangered species. As it has been widely documented, it can also disrupt wildlife behaviour, such as, tourist vehicles in Africa's national parks that approach wild cats and thus distract them from hunting and breeding; tour boat operators in the Caribbean Sea that feed sharks to ensure that they remain in tourist areas; and whale-watching boat crews around the world that pursue whales and dolphins and even encourage petting, which tends to alter the animals' feeding and behaviour.

Tourism can also lead to the indiscriminate clearance of native vegetation for the development of new facilities, increased demand for fuelwood and even forest fires. Ecologically fragile areas, such as rain forests, wetlands and mangroves, are also threatened by intensive or irresponsible tourist activity. Moreover, as will be discussed below, it is increasingly recognized that, the rapid expansion of nature tourism may also pose a threat to ecologically fragile areas, including natural world heritage sites, if not properly managed and monitored. In many countries, coastlines are becoming overbuilt due to tourism development until the damage caused by environmental degradation – and the eventual loss of revenues arising from a collapse in tourism arrivals – becomes irreversible.

Intensive tourism development and recreational activities in coastal areas can not only lead to beach destruction and coastal degradation, but can also threaten coral reefs and other marine ecosystems. The delicate ecosystems of most small islands, together with their increasing reliance on tourism as a main tool of socioeconomic development, means that these environmental impacts can be particularly damaging since the success of the sector in these islands often depends on the quality of their natural environment. In addition, pollution of coastal waters – in particular by sewage, solid waste, sediments and untreated chemicals – often leads to the deterioration of coastal ecosystems, notably coral reefs, and thus harms their value for tourism.

One of the most serious environmental problems in mountainous developing countries without appropriate energy supply is deforestation arising from increasing consumption of fuelwood by the tourism industry. This often results not only in the destruction of local habitats and ecosystems, but also in accelerating processes of erosion and landslides. Other major problems arising from tourist activities in mountain regions include disruption of animal migration by road and tourist facilities, sewage pollution of rivers, excessive water withdrawals from streams to supply resorts and accumulation of solid waste on trails.

There is now plenty of evidence of the 'life-cycle' of a tourist destination, that is, its evolution from discovery, to development, to eventual decline, attributed to a site's overuse and the subsequent deterioration of key attractions or facilities. In other words, the negative impacts of intensive tourism activities on the environmental quality of beaches, mountains, rivers, forests and other ecosystems also compromise the viability of the tourism industry in these places. Tourism in many destinations could be particularly threatened by global environmental problems, notably the potential threat of 'global warming'. There is increasing scientific evidence that human activity has begun to change the average temperature on the Earth's surface.

According to the authoritative United Nations Intergovernmental Panel on Climate Change (IPCC), this process of global warming has been caused by several factors associated with the intensification of economic activities, including the emissions of 'greenhouse gases', such as carbon dioxide produced by burning fossil fuels and forests. According to the Third Assessment Report of

IPCC, it is expected that the globally averaged surface air temperature will have warmed between 1. 4 and 5. 8 degrees Celsius by 2100 relative to 1990. One of the main consequences of global warming will be sea-level rise: according to IPCC, it is projected that the globally averaged sea level will have risen between 9 and almost 90 centimetres by 2100.

Global warming is also expected to increase climate variability and to provoke changes in the frequency and intensity of extreme climate events, such as tropical windstorms and associated storm surges and coastal flooding. Significant rises in sea level could cause serious problems to tourism activities, particularly in low-lying coastal areas and small islands. According to IPCC, because of their high degree of environmental vulnerability, small island States are likely to be among the countries most seriously affected by global warming. Severe negative impacts on coastal ecosystems, such as bleaching of coral reefs and deterioration of mangroves, are also expected to threaten tourism in many destinations around the world. In fact, global warming is expected to severely disrupt tourism activities not only in coastal areas and small islands, but also in mountain regions because snow conditions in ski resorts are likely to become less reliable.

Sustainable Tourism Development

Tourism in today's world finds it necessary to manipulate and modify the environment to suit its purpose. Tourism certainly can contribute to environmental degradation and be self-destructive; it also has potential to bring about significant enhancement of the environment. With tourism-induced change, an Important issue, for example, is irreversibility, which in part is a function of the resilience of the resource base, along with the spatial and temporal pattern of impacts, and the scope for compensatory managerial response. An influential conference held in Canada on 'Global opportunities for business and the environment' concluded that sustainable development holds considerable promise as a vehicle for addressing the problems of modern tourism. Clearly, what seems to be occur ring is recognition of the interdependence between environmental and economic issues and policies, and ultimately, acceptance of the notion that sound environmental management in tourism does not merely cost, it pays. Of course, convincing decision makers of the good sense, both environmentally and commercially, of the merits of a sustainable approach to tourism may not be easy. It can be difficult to demonstrate conclusively the costs over time of environmental degradation, especially when set against the more immediate returns forgone by adopting a more restrained pattern of development.

The tourism industry of the 1990s is showing commendable preparedness to apply the principles of best practice environmental management to its activities, especially at the largerscale, corporate level. If the process of achieving sustainable forms of development in a growing tourism industry is a formidable challenge, the task takes on additional dimensions when set against the many forces for change facing the industry as it moves into the next century.

New spatial forms and settings must be anticipated as tourist developers seek to service a diverse and expanding array of interests and opportunities. Tourism can be a very volatile industry, sensitive to changes in perception and taste, and to altered biophysical, economic or political circumstances.Thus the theme of change is constant on the tourism scene. In a business sense, the professional component of tourism is constrained to keep abreast of change, and be aware of, and respond to changes in travel preferences, in technology, and in the many factors which help fashion 19 the travel market. A danger is that in these circumstances, sustainability may only be pursued in a financial or business management context. Ecologically sustainable tourism development may be seen as too expensive and irrelevant to business success. Much research interest focuses on the responses of tourists and tourism to changing socioeconomic circumstances, to political., cultural and attitudinal changes to improvements in spatial awareness and communication, and to growing environmental concern for sustainability. In almost five decades since the resurgence of organized travel in 1948, tourism, as an international phenomenon, has passed through different stages until it has become a gigantic instrument in the develop mental strategy of a good number of countries.

As expressed by the World Tourism Organisation, tourism is ambivalent. It can contribute positively to socioeconomic and cultural achievements, while at the same time it may cause the degradation of environment and the loss of local identity. It should therefore be approached with a global methodology. It is incumbent upon the destination to orient its tourism growth towards meeting its socioeconomic objectives and environmental requirements. Moreover, tourism growth must coincide with the destination's prevailing value system and cultural integrity, and satisfy the needs of its local population.

The term sustainability, which has gained prominence in tourism jargon, is seen by many writers as an important part of the philosophy permeating all levels of tourism policy issues and practice from national to local. Others understand sustainability as a deep-rooted concept that relates to the fundamentals of life which sometimes are obscured by the ongoing public/private debate, regulation and rationalized government intervention. Needless to say sustainable development and management of tourism resources should coincide with economic, sociocultural, nealth, safety and environmental objectives at national, regional and local levels.

The World Tourism Organisation (WTO) defined sustainable tourism development as that

> which meets the needs of present tourists and host regions while protecting and enhancing opportunity for the future. It is envisaged as leading to the management of all resources in such a way that economic, social and aesthetic needs can be fulfilled while maintaining cultural integrity, essential ecological processes, biological diversity and life support systems.

Tourism is no longer a soft option. On the contrary, due to multiple variables intervening, it is becoming a rather complicated developmental sector which requires expertise and professionalism. Tourism's multifaceted function, as a socioeconomic and politico-cultural phenomenon, as a complex industry, and as a profession having its own rules and code of ethics, requires a broad intellectual background and specialized education and/or training to enable its policy makers and professionals to keep abreast of the scientific and technological changes. If we just think of the various organizational, marketing planning and technical aspects of tourism, we must realize how complex round tourism development is.The old classical approach to tourism problem-solving through day-to-day tactics can no longer hold good in the face of a rapidly growing and swiftly changing world tourism industry.

While tourism has become increasingly appreciated as a contributor to he national economics of some leading tourist destinations, lack of sufficient information about the scope and essence of that activity as well as of the processes linked to it are still widespread. It is important, however, to ask what alternative forms of tourism prove to be sustainable and which do not. Some forms of tourism are considered by some writers as sustainable, such as ecotourism and special interest tourism, although as yet no empirical research has proved such claims.The crucial question in this connection is whether tourism sustainability, at least within the narrow confines of some alternative tourism forms, could be a reality. The answer to the above question is positive. Yes, tourism sustainability could be a reality. It is the by-product of a multitude of factors that contribute to the successful present integration and future continuity of tourism it the macro and micro levels in destinations.

As all socioeconomic, vultural, political and environmental factors and subject to change in time and space, sustainability is therefore a relative term and not an absolute fact. Markets, fashions, tastes, motivations, images, trends and destinations are all likely to change, at least in the long term. Thus tourism has to be humane and adaptive to the needs of the tourists, responsive to the needs of local communities, socioeconomically and culturally well planned, and environmentally sound. The difficulty is to determine how tourism can protect and enhance opportunities for future generations of tourists and host communities while change continues to prevail. This is the challenge that tourism sustainability has to face and surmount. Such challenge manifests itself in evolving tourist behavioural patterns and forms, progress in host community attitudes towards tourism, and change in technology and marketing opportunities. Tourism must offer products that are operated in harmony with the local environment, community attitudes and cultures, so that these become the permanent beneficiaries and not the victims of tourism development.

Sustainable Tourism: Programmes and Policies

Governments can influence the development of tourism in certain areas by setting the conditions of investments and the scope of financial concessions, and regulating conditions of access to land, for example by allowing only long-term leases or rights of usufruct on land for foreign investors. Some governments still play an important role in providing infrastructure for tourism development, and also include tourism in their development strategies and land use plans.

State involvement in the orientation, regulation and reasonable control of the tourism industry might be deemed necessary to attain a growth rate which is regarded by governments as desirable and sometimes necessary. Such a growth rate would be higher than the market-driven rate. If past, present and future are connected by a time continuum, change, as previously mentioned, may separate these time dimensions, creating phases of different actions, reactions and outcomes. However, these would be inter related by the forces of cause and effect. Therefore sustainability and balanced tourism growth could be deemed as two intimately related concepts.

Selective growth and striking a balance between tourist supply and demand, between attractions, facilities and services, between quantity and quality, between number of arrivals and natural, social and cultural carrying capacities, are some safeguards against mismanagement of tourism. These safeguards, among other policy decisions, would lead to sustainability and avoidance or mitigation of various detriments to tourism.

Agenda 21 is a comprehensive programme of action adopted by governments at the 1992 United Nations Conference on Environment and Development (UNCED), known as the Earth Summit. It provides a blueprint for securing the sustainable future of the planet into the twenty first century and is the first document of its kind to achieve widespread international agreement and commitment to work harmoniously towards the conservation of the earth's natural resources. The travel and tourism industry is considered the world's largest industry, generating in 1905 an estimated US$3.4 trillion in gross output, creating employment for more than 211 million people, producing 10.9 per cent of world gross domestic product (GDP), investing $693.9 billion in new facilities and equipment, and contributing more than $637 billion to global tax revenue. By the year 2005 it is estimated that the industry will have expanded its global role, generating $7.2 trillion in gross output, creating employment for 305 million people, producing 11.4 per cent of world GDP, investing $1,613 billion in new facilities and equipment, and contributing more than $1,369 billion in tax revenue. With this privileged position in the world economy, the travel and tourism industry should be recognized as a world leader in contributing to sustainable development.

However, Agenda 21 did not mention travel and tourism except in a few sections. Coastal states should explore the scope for expanding recreation and tourist activities based in marine living resources; Countries should 'promote, as appropriate, environmentally sound leisure and tourism activities... making suitable use of museums, heritage sites, zoos, botanical gardens, national parks, and other protected areas' Strict adherence to the promotion of nature-oriented, specialized, humanistic and low-capacity tourism to bring about environmental quality, improvement, while sound in itself, cannot live up to the promise of realizing the industry's huge expectations for worldwide improved expansion. The real benefits lie in making all forms of travel and tourism sustainable this is the real challenge facing all travel and tourism policy makers and industry professionals.

Some key objectives to be achieved in the next ten years are as follows:

— Create socioeconomic value for primitive resources including natural beauty, wildlife, wilderness and forests as well as historical and cultural heritage, built heritage and traditional ways of life.

— Offer sufficient incentives and provide means for environmental enhancement of urban areas, especially in industrial cities.

— Provide necessary infrastructure in remote areas with tourism potential, to encourage human settlements and other economic activities to grow in harmony with tourism.

— Research and develop environmentally compatible technology that could lead to socioeconomic growth and culturally oriented advancement.

— Use international communication networks to spread messages and practices of sustainable development.

Implementation of Agenda 21 requires a major shift in priorities, involving a full integration of sustainable development considerations into economic and social policies, and a major redeployment of human and financial resources at national and international levels. In many cases there will be significant benefits from this shift; governments will spend less on health-care and face lower cleanup costs; businesses will experience cost saving from more efficient resource use; tourism destinations will enjoy long-term success; and finally our children will be guaranteed a sustainable future. This joint document translates the Agenda into an action programme for the travel and tourism industry which aims at helping national tourist administrations (NTAs), representative trade organizations and travel and tourism companies fulfil their potential to achieve sustainable development through tourism.

Travel and tourism can transform the following key objectives into reality in the medium and long term:

— Create economic value for resources where utilization and exploitation would, in principle, yield no returns. These are natural and cultural resources such as forests, wilderness, wildlife, archaeological sites, cultural heritage and modern built heritage.

— Provide good reasons and means for environmental conservation of areas which are in need of such environmental awareness. These are mainly large cities centres and old industrial sites.

— Create employment opportunities in various regions arid localities suit able for tourism development.

— Extend necessary tourist infrastructure and superstructure to remote and depressed areas, helping to stimulate economic activities in those areas.

— Use modern communications media to transfer experiences and practices of sustainable development between nations, particularly from developed to developing countries.

— Provide examples to other industries in the adoption of business practices that contribute to sustainable development and lead ideas on sound environmental management.

Tourism adopts a different perspective that should be compatible, for all practical purposes, with the environment and the community in which it is active. Environmental and societal systems cannot realistically exist in an operational vacuum, but mostly coexist with judicious economic development, and address relevant needs of the host community in the same global system.

Many environmentalists, however, seem to ignore or be unaware of this precondition. This is another issue that confirms the necessity to subscribe to an integrated systemic approach that resides in well conceived policy which should be properly implemented in order to guarantee sustainability. A necessary national dialogue on sustainable tourism would result in multi various policy directives to guide appropriate action within the context of respective mandates and capabilities. In the present context it is sufficient to deal with policy determinants that relate to the government as a whole, while acknowledging other tourism industry players' share of policy.

International Guidelines for Sustainable Tourism

The International Guidelines for activities related to sustainable tourism development are intended to assist Parties to the Convention on Biological Diversity, public authorities and stakeholders at all levels, to apply the provisions of the Convention to the sustainable development and management of tourism activities. They will provide technical guidance to policy makers, decision makers and managers with responsibilities covering tourism and/or biodiversity, whether in national or local government, the private sector, indigenous and local communities, non governmental organizations or other organizations, on ways of working together with key stakeholders involved in tourism and biodiversity in order to contribute, inter alia, to functioning ecosystems; sustainable tourism in functioning ecosystems; fair and equitable sharing of benefits; information and capacity-building; restoration of past damage.

While the guidelines were developed focusing on vulnerable terrestrial, marine and coastal ecosystems and habitats of major importance for biological diversity and protected areas, they are appropriate for tourism and biological diversity in all areas. Governments, international institutions and development agencies should take these guidelines into account in their policies, programmes and activities, and support their implementation, especially in developing countries and should encourage the exchange of experiences and lessons learned concerning their implementation.

A Broad Scope

The guidelines cover all forms and activities of tourism, which should all come under the framework of sustainable development, in all geographic regions. These include, but are not limited to, conventional mass tourism, ecotourism, nature- and culture-based tourism, cruise tourism, leisure and sports tourism.

Management

Management should be based on a consultative process involving multi-stakeholder participation.

The management process needs to be undertaken through a multi-stakeholder process. Governments will normally coordinate this process at national level. This process may also be undertaken at more local levels and at community level. It is important for Governments to consult with and involve all relevant stakeholders ensuring strong involvement of indigenous and local communities throughout the management process, including decision-making on use of biodiversity resources.

Interdepartmental and inter-organizational structures and processes should be established to ensure coordination to guide policy development and implementation and to improve awareness and exchange of knowledge among stakeholders at all levels. A consultative process, based on multi-stakeholder participation, should be established to ensure ongoing and effective dialogue and information sharing and the stakeholder engagement and participation in the whole process. The establishment of partnerships should be encouraged.

Ten steps for management

The management process comprises ten steps for management of sustainable tourism and biodiversity:

1. Baseline information and review;
2. Vision and goals;
3. Objectives;
4. Review of legislation and control measures;
5. Impact assessment;
6. Impact management;
7. Decision making;
8. Implementation;
9. Monitoring;
10. Adaptive management.

Baseline information and review

Baseline information enables informed decision making and impact assessment.

Its compilation should follow the ecosystem approach. For tourism and biodiversity, the baseline information could include information at national and local levels on current economic, social and environmental conditions, considering also the structure and trends within the tourism sector and an account of benefits from, and costs of, tourism to local communities. Information on damage done to the environment in the past, environmental and biodiversity resources, including any special features and sites of particular importance and culturally sensitive areas could also be provided in this phase of the process. National biodiversity strategies, action plans and reports and national, subnational and local sustainable-development plans are also a good source of baseline information.

Information for consideration as part of baseline information includes traditional knowledge as well as scientific information. All relevant stakeholders may contribute information to this process, including biodiversity managers and indigenous and local communities. Collation and synthesis of information provided will need to be undertaken by an appropriately qualified team, drawing on a range of expertise. Together with the Government which typically assumes the responsibility of the exercise, all stakeholders should be involved in review of the collated baseline information available, and in the synthesis of this information.

The baseline information gathering and review process should make full use of the clearing-house mechanism under the Convention on Biological Diversity, as well as of relevant networks such as the World Network of Biosphere Reserves, World Heritage sites and Ramsar sites.

Vision and goals

An overall vision and goals is important for the effective management of tourism and biodiversity, and for ensuring that it contributes to poverty alleviation.

The vision and goals take into account national and regional sustainable development plans for economic and social development and for land-use, as well as the baseline information and review. The main vision and goals are established to seek to maximize the positive benefits of tourism on biodiversity, ecosystems, and economic and social development, while minimizing negative social and environmental impacts from tourism. They can cover economic and planning matters (i.e. sharing of benefits, integration and diversification of activities, zoning and control of development), ecological and scientific matters (i.e. function of ecosystems, biodiversity conservation and sustainable use), social concerns (i.e. poverty alleviation, protection of indigenous resources, participation and involvement of indigenous and local communities), and dissemination of information and capacity building.

The vision and goals will form the basis of national strategies or master plans for sustainable development of tourism in relation to biodiversity, and vice versa. Governments should take into account local and community level visions and goals when preparing the national level visions and goals.

Objectives

The objectives focus on actions to implement the overall vision and goals.

The objectives may include clear targets, a timetable for their achievement and details of areas where tourism development and activities are potential development options, including details of the type and scale of such development and activities that would be acceptable and impact management measures that would be appropriate.

Governments should provide national planning frameworks and planning guidance to ensure that developments or activities are not undertaken outside areas set out in the objectives. Previous to any developments, analysis of market conditions and trends should be carried out to check the viability of the market.

Governments may also wish to consider measures to establish and support conservation areas, by:

(a) ensuring appropriate legal recognition to designated areas;

(b) establishing reserves based on the biosphere reserve concept;

(c) strengthening the protected area network;

(d) using economic policy tools and encouraging the private sector to actively support conservation efforts.

Review of legislation and control measures

Legislation and appropriate regulatory mechanisms and tools are essential for the effective implementation of any overall vision, goals, and objectives.

A review of legislation and control measures (such as land-use planning, environmental assessment, building regulations and standards for tourism) may be necessary to update and further develop legislation and control measures. Such a review could include provisions for increasing indigenous and local communities land-management, access and ownership, decision-making on issues related to tourism development, and activities and for increasing collective rights.

Legislation and control measures considered could include approval and licensing for tourism development and activities, incentives for sustainable tourism and the application of economic instruments for the management of tourism and biodiversity. The control of the planning and siting of tourism facilities and the establishment of infrastructures could also be considered and addressed by the legislation. In this context, integrated land use management and environmental assessment could be used to develop policies and measure their impacts.

Impact assessment

Impact assessment includes assessment of the environmental, social, cultural, economic effects, both positive and negative, of proposed developments.

Governments are encouraged to develop mechanisms for impact assessment with the participation of all stakeholders, including nature conservation bodies, and to ensure effective implementation of existing mechanisms. Comprehensive impact assessments are important for all tourism developments and activities, and should take into account cumulative effects from multiple development activities of all types at all levels. Governments, through appropriately qualified teams, will normally undertake evaluations of the adequacy of impact assessments submitted by proposers of tourism developments or activities. If the information provided is not sufficient, or the impact assessment inadequate, then further impact assessment studies may need to be undertaken.

Indigenous and local communities concerned should be fully involved in impact assessment, which should also recognize the contribution of traditional knowledge in the development, implementation and review of appropriate and effective methodologies and criteria to be used for impact assessment.

Impacts of tourism in relation to the environment and biological diversity may include analysis of land-use, consumption and depletion of local natural resources, considering damages and alterations to habitats and ecosystems. Impact assessment could also consider contamination and pollution from different sources due to tourism activities, deterioration of resources, production of waste and the introduction of alien species and pathogens. Socio-economic and cultural impacts on different segments of the population should also be considered, including social degradation of local communities, impact on traditional practices and lifestyles, incomes and jobs.

The potential benefits of tourism may include the creation of revenues for the maintenance of natural areas and contribution to economic development, through the creation of new infrastructures and services, jobs and the provision of funds, as well as the through the diversification of the economy.

Impact management

Impact management is essential to avoid or minimize any potential damage to biodiversity conservation and sustainable use that tourism development or activities might cause.

To be sustainable, tourism should be managed within the carrying capacity and limits of acceptable change for ecosystem and sites, and to ensure that tourism activities contribute to the conservation of biodiversity. Tourism should be restricted, and where necessary prevented, in ecologically sensitive areas.

Proposals for tourism development or activities may incorporate proposals for impact management. Impact management can include measures for the siting of tourism development and activities and measures to control tourist flows in and around tourist destinations and key sites, to promote appropriate behavior by tourists so as to minimize their impacts, and to establish limits to numbers of visitors and their impacts within carrying capacity / limits to acceptable change at any site.

Impact management for tourism development and activities can include the adoption of policies, good practices and lessons learned that cover different areas of interest. The control and reduction of impact from tourist flows and activities and the minimization and prevention of pollution and waste should be addressed to minimize negative effects on destinations. The sound planning and design of facilities, services and technologies could also be addressed through the promotion of eco-efficiency, the cleaner production approach, the conservation of landscapes and natural and cultural heritages, and the preparation of contingency plans for environmental emergencies. Impact management could include policies, good practices and lessons learned on conservation and responsible use of natural resources, and considerations on local communities involvement and participation, respecting the integrity of local cultures and the use of local products and skills. Public Education and Awareness could also be included in impact management policies, for the promotion of appropriate behaviors, alignment of marketing strategies, environmental and cultural sustainability audits.

The tourism industry can assist in promoting wide implementation of management measures for sustainable tourism and the conservation and sustainable use of biodiversity in relation to tourism.

Decision making

Decision making should be a transparent and accountable process to approve or refuse a proposal, and it should always apply to the precautionary principle.

Decisions regarding tourism and biodiversity will be made concerning approval or otherwise of national strategies and plans for tourism and biodiversity, proposals for tourism development and activities and the adequacy of impact management measures in relation to anticipated impacts from tourism development and activities. Decisions will be taken ultimately by Governments (or specific authorities designated by them). Effective consultation with and participation of the communities and groups affected is an important foundation of the decision-making process. Decision makers should consider using multi-stakeholder processes as a tool for this.

Legal mechanisms should be put in place for notification and approval of tourism development proposals and for ensuring implementation of the conditions of approval of development proposals.

Decision-making should include the prior informed consent of indigenous and local communities affected by projects in order to ensure respect for the customs and traditional knowledge, innovations and practices of indigenous and local communities. Adequate funding and technical support should be provided for these groups to participate effectively.

In making a decision, conditions may be attached to any approvals that may be granted, including conditions regarding management of tourism in relation to avoidance or minimization of adverse impacts on biodiversity, and for appropriate decommissioning of tourism activities should the development cease. Decision makers may also, as appropriate, request further information from a proposer; defer a decision pending further baseline research by other agencies; or refuse a proposal.

Implementation

Implementation follows a decision to approve a particular proposal, strategy or plan, and must include implementation of all conditions that may have been set for granting of approval.

The developer and/or operator will be responsible for complying with these conditions and they can also be required to notify the designated government authority of any failures to comply with conditions attached to an approval. Any revisions or changes to an approved project, including additions and/or variations of activities, must be approved by the designated authorities. Local stakeholders should be given an ongoing opportunity to express their wishes and concerns to those managing tourism facilities and activities, based on clear, adequate and accessible information.

Governments and designated authorities will need to monitor compliance with, and enforce as necessary, conditions attached to any approval. Communities and other interested stakeholders may also monitor compliance and report their findings to the designated government authorities.

Monitoring

Monitoring and surveillance in relation to management of tourism and biodiversity includes the compliance of implementation of approved tourism developments or activities, the monitoring of the impacts of tourism activities on biodiversity and ecosystems and on surrounding population and the monitoring of general tourism activities and trends.

Developers and operators of tourism facilities and activities may be required to report periodically to designated authorities and to the public, on compliance with conditions set out in approvals, and on the condition of biodiversity and the environment in relation to the tourism facilities and activities for which they are responsible.

An inclusive monitoring and reporting system should be put in place, prior to commencement of any new tourism development or activities providing for the involvement of indigenous and local communities at all stages. Indicators to cover all aspects of management of biodiversity and sustainable tourism, including socioeconomic and cultural aspects, should be identified and selected at national and tourist destination levels.

Monitoring and surveillance in relation to biodiversity impacts should include activities undertaken to ensure respect for endangered species under relevant international agreements, prevention of introduction of alien species, compliance with national and international rules concerning access to genetic resources, and prevention of illegal and unauthorized removal of genetic resources.

Monitoring and evaluation should also include development and use of appropriate tools to monitor and evaluate tourism impacts on the economy of indigenous and local communities. Use of indicators and early warning systems should be developed as appropriate, taking into account traditional knowledge, innovation and practices of indigenous and local communities, and guidelines developed under the Convention on Biological Diversity relating to traditional knowledge.

Long-term monitoring and assessment is necessary in relation to the impacts of tourism on biodiversity, and will need to take into account the timescale for ecosystem changes to become evident. Monitoring of general environmental and biodiversity conditions and trends, as well as tourism trends and impacts, can be undertaken by governments, including designated biodiversity managers. Management measures may need to be adjusted, as appropriate, where adverse impacts on biodiversity and ecosystems are detected.

Adaptive management

Adaptive management deals with the complex and dynamic nature of ecosystems and the absence of complete knowledge or understanding of their functioning.

Ecosystem processes are often nonlinear, the outcome of such processes often shows time-lags and their level of uncertainty is increased by the interaction with social construct. Management must be adaptive in order to be able to respond to such uncertainties and contain elements of "learning-by-doing" or research feedback.

Ecosystem management must involve a learning process, which helps to adapt methodologies and practices to the ways in which these systems are being managed and monitored. Adaptive management should also take the precautionary principle fully into account. There is also a need for flexibility in policy-making and implementation. Long-term, inflexible decisions are likely to be inadequate or even destructive. Ecosystem management should be envisaged as a long-term experiment that builds on its results as it progresses.

Implementing adaptive management in relation to tourism and biodiversity will require the active cooperation and close interaction of tourism managers and biodiversity managers. Governments in conjunction with all other stakeholders and those who have management control over any specific site, will need to take actions to address any problems encountered and to keep on track towards agreed goals. Adaptive management can also be undertaken by all those who have management control over any specific site, including local government, indigenous and local communities, the private sector, non-governmental organizations and other organizations.

Notification Proccess and Information Requirements

Proposals for tourism development and activities at particular locations in relation to biodiversity, are to be submitted through the notification process.

Proposers of tourism projects, including government agencies, should provide full and timely advance notice to relevant authorities and all stakeholders who may be affected, including indigenous and local communities, of proposed developments through a formal process of prior informed approval. Considerations on the development site could include geographical description and location and its proximity to human settlements and communities and laws and regulations applicable. Economic considerations could cover the analysis of the market for proposed tourism development and activities, the description of current socioeconomic conditions and the expected changes. Ecological aspects of the site and its surroundings should include an analysis of flora, fauna and ecosystems that could be affected and the impact on local communities as well as possible transboundary effects and impacts.

Information provided should be made public, and public comment invited on all proposals for tourism development and activities.

Government response to notification of proposals for tourism development may range from approvals, with or without conditions, to refusal of the proposal. Further information from the proposer and further research by other agencies may be requested by Governments.

Publication and Awareness Raising

Public education and awareness raising campaigns need to be addressed to both the professional sectors and the general public to inform them about the impacts of tourism on biological diversity, and good practices in this area.

Public awareness campaigns will need to be tailored for various audiences, particularly stakeholders including consumers of tourism, developers and tourism operators. The private sector could play an active role encouraging conservation among clients.

Education and awareness-raising is required at all levels of government. Awareness should also be increased within and outside governments that vulnerable ecosystems and habitats are often located within lands and waters occupied or used by indigenous and local communities. It is also important to raise awareness within the academic sector responsible for training and research on issues regarding the harmonious interaction between biological diversity and sustainable tourism.

Capapcity Building

Capacity-building activities should aim to develop and strengthen the capacities of governments and all stakeholders to facilitate the effective implementation of these guidelines, and may be necessary at local, national, regional and international levels. Capacity-building activities can include strengthening human resources and institutional capacities; the transfer of know-how; the development of appropriate facilities; training in relation to biological diversity and sustainable tourism issues, and impact assessment and impact management techniques. Local communities should also be equipped with the necessary decision-making abilities, skills and knowledge in advance of future tourist in-flows, as well as with relevant capacity and training regarding tourism services and environmental protection.

Capacity-building activities should provide assistance to stakeholders in undertaking all the steps of the management processes and in strengthening mechanisms for impact assessment. Capacity-building should also include the establishment of multistakeholder processes and the training of tourism professionals.

Information exchange and collaboration regarding sustainable tourism implementation through networking and partnerships between all stakeholders affected by, or involved in tourism, including the private sector, should be encouraged.

Charter of Sustainable Tourism

We, the participants at the World Conference on Sustainable Tourism, meeting in Lanzarote, Canary Islands, Spain, on 27-28 April 1995,

Mindful that tourism, as a worldwide phenomenon, touches the highest and deepest aspirations of all people and is also an important element of socioeconomic and political development in many countries.

Recognizing that tourism is ambivalent, since it can contribute positively to socio-economic and cultural achievement, while at the same time it can contribute to the degradation of the environment and the loss of local identity, and should therefore be approached with a global methodology.

Mindful that the resources on which tourism is based are fragile and that there is a growing demand for improved environmental quality.

Recognizing that tourism affords the opportunity to travel and to know other cultures, and that the development of tourism can help promote closer ties and peace among peoples, creating a conscience that is respectful of the diversity of culture and life styles.

Recalling the Universal Declaration of Human Rights, adopted by the General Assembly of United Nations, and the various United Nations declarations and regional conventions on tourism, the environment, the conservation of cultural heritage and on sustainable development.

Guided by the principles set forth in the Rio Declaration on the Environment and Development and the recommendations arising from Agenda 21.

Recalling previous declarations on tourism, such as the Manila Declaration on World Tourism, the Hague Declaration and the Tourism Bill of Rights and Tourist Code.

Recognizing the need to develop a tourism that meets economic expectations and environmental requirements, and respects not only the social and physical structure of destinations, but also the local population.

Considering it a priority to protect and reinforce the human dignity of both local communities and tourists. Mindful of the need to establish effective alliances among the principal actors in the field of tourism so as to fulfil the hope of a tourism that is more responsible towards our common heritage.

APPEAL to the international community and, in particular, URGE governments, other public authorities, decisionmakers and professionals in the field of tourism, public and private associations and institutions whose activities are related to tourism, and tourists themselves, to adopt the principles and objectives of the Declaration that follows:

1. Tourism development shall be based on criteria of sustainability, which means that it must be ecologically bearable in the long term, as well as economically viable, and ethically and socially equitable for local communities. Sustainable development is a guided process which envisages global management of resources so as to ensure their viability, thus enabling our natural and cultural capital, including protected areas, to be preserved. As a powerful instrument of development, tourism can and should participate actively in the sustainable development strategy. A requirement of sound management of tourism is that the sustainability of the resources on which it depends must be guaranteed.

2. Tourism should contribute to sustainable development and be integrated with the natural, cultural and human environment; it must respect the fragile balances that characterize many tourist destinations, in particular small islands and environmentally sensitive areas. Tourism should ensure an acceptable evolution as regards its influence on natural resources, biodiversity and the capacity for assimilation of any impacts and residues produced.

3. Tourism must consider its effects on the cultural heritage and traditional elements, activities and dynamics of each local community. Recognition of these local factors and support for the identity, culture and interests of the local community must at all times play a central role in the formulation of tourism strategies, particularly in developing countries.

4. The active contribution of tourism to sustainable development necessarily presupposes the solidarity, mutual respect and participation of all the actors, both public and private, implicated in the process, and must be based on efficient cooperation mechanisms at all levels: local, national, regional and international.

5. The conservation, protection and appreciation of the worth of the natural and cultural heritage afford a privileged area for cooperation. This approach implies that all those responsible must take upon themselves a true challenge, that of cultural, technological and professional innovation, and must also undertake a major effort to create and implement integrated planning and management instruments.

6. Quality criteria both for the preservation of the tourist destination and for the capacity to satisfy tourists, determined jointly with local communities and informed by the principles of sustainable development, should represent priority objectives in the formulation of tourism strategies and projects.

7. To participate in sustainable development, tourism must be based on the diversity of opportunities offered by the local economy. It should be fully integrated into and contribute positively to local economic development.

8. All options for tourism development must serve effectively to improve the quality of life of all people and must influence the socio-cultural enrichment of each destination.

9. Governments and the competent authorities, with the participation of NGOs and local communities, shall

undertake actions aimed at integrating the planning of tourism as a contribution to sustainable development.

10. In recognition of economic and social cohesion among the peoples of the world as a fundamental principle of sustainable development, it is urgent that measures be promoted to permit a more equitable distribution of the benefits and burdens of tourism. This implies a change of consumption patterns and the introduction of pricing methods which allow environmental costs to be internalised. Governments and multilateral organizations should prioritize and strengthen direct and indirected aid to tourism projects which contribute to improving the quality of the environment. Within this context, it is necessary to explore thoroughly the application of internationally harmonised economic, legal and fiscal instruments tc ensure the sustainable use of resources in tourism.

11. Environmentally and culturally vulnerable spaces, both now and in the future, shall be given special priority in the matter of technical cooperation and financial aid for sustainable tourism development. Similarly, special treatment should be given to zones that have been degraded by obsolete and high impact tourism models.

12. The promotion of alternative forms of tourism that are compatible with the principles of sustainable development, together with the encouragement of diversification represent a guarantee of stability in the medium and the long term. In this respect there is a need, for many small islands and environmentally sensitive areas in particular, to actively pursue and strengthen regional cooperation.

13. Governments, industry, authorities, and tourism-related NGOs should promote and participate in the creation of open networks for research, dissemination of information and transfer of appropriate knowledge on tourism and environmentally sustainable tourism technologies.

14. The establishment of a sustainable tourism policy necessarily requires the support and promotion of environmentally-compatible tourism management systems, feasibility studies for the transformation of the sector, as well as the implementation of demonstration projects and the development of international cooperation programmes.

15. The travel industry, together with bodies and NGOs whose activities are related to tourism, shall draw up specific frameworks for positive and preventive actions to secure sustainable tourism development and establish programmes to support the implementation of such practices. They shall monitor achievements, report on results and exchange their experiences.

16. Particular attention should be paid to the role and the environmental repercussions of transport in tourism, and to the development of economic instruments designed to reduce the use of non-renewable energy and to encourage recycling and minimization of residues in resorts.

17. The adoption and implementation of codes of conduct conducive to sustainability by the principal actors involved in tourism, particularly industry, are fundamental if tourism is to be sustainable. Such codes can be effective instruments for the development of responsible tourism activities.

18. All necessary measures should be implemented in order to inform and promote awareness among all parties involved in the tourism industry, at local, national, regional and international level, with regard to the contents and objectives of the Lanzarote Conference.

7

Tourism: Demands and Expectations

Tourism demands

Tourism is primarily a demand-side oriented concept, i.e. oriented by those persons engaging in tourism. These persons are called visitors. The term 'visitors' comprises tourists and same-day visitors. The term visitor describes: "any person travelling to a place other than that of his/her usual environment for less than twelve consecutive months and whose main purpose of travel is other than the exercise of an activity remunerated from within the place visited".

The three fundamental criteria that appear sufficient to distinguish visitors from other travellers are as follows:

i) the trip should be to a place other than that of the usual environment,

ii) the stay in the place visited should not last more than twelve consecutive months,

iii) the main purpose of the visit should be other than the exercise of an activity remunerated from within the place visited.

The usual environment - The usual environment of a person consists of the direct vicinity of his/her home and place of work or study and other places frequently visited. The concept of usual environment and therefore tourism, has two dimensions:

— *Frequency:* places which are frequently visited by a person are considered as part of their usual environment even though these places may be located at a considerable distance from the place of residence.

— *Distance:* places located close to the place of residence of a person are also part of the usual environment even if the actual spots are rarely visited.

Length of stay - usual residence: The second criterion is that visitors should not stay 12 consecutive months or more in the place visited. This is in fact an extension of the usual environment concept, since if a person resides within an area during 12 consecutive months, this area can be considered to have become his/her "usual environment". A person staying or intending to stay one year or more in a given area is considered a resident of that place and therefore not a visitor from the point of view of tourism statistics.

Resident in a country/in a place : for the purposes of international/domestic tourism statistics, a person is considered to be a resident in a country/place if he/she:has lived for most of the past year (12 months) in that country/place, or has lived in that country/place for a shorter period and intends to return within 12 months to live in that country/place.

The place/country of usual residence determines whether a person arriving in a region/country is a visitor or other traveller, as well as that person's origin. The underlying concept in the classification of international visitors by places of origin is the country of residence, not their citizenship/nationality. Foreign citizens residing in a country are assimilated to other residents for the purpose of domestic and outbound tourism statistics. Citizens of a country residing abroad who return to their home country on a temporary visit are included among non-resident visitors, though it may be desirable to distinguish them in some studies.

Remuneration from the within the place visited: The third criterion is that the main purpose of the visit should be other than the exercise of an activity remunerated from within the place visited. The term "remuneration" refers to payments which cover the reward for labour, i.e. wages and salaries (including payment in kind) and not travel allowances or small participation fees.

Origin and destination : trip and stay - Whatever form or category of tourism is studied, we can have an origin-based or a destination-based perspective. To distinguish the two it is recommended to use the term "trip" to describe tourism from the standpoint of the generating place or country (the origin) and "stay" to describe tourism from the standpoint of the receiving place or country (the destination or place visited). The "trip" covers the whole period during which the person engages in tourism, while the "stay" covers only part of it.

The volume and character of tourism depend on the point of measurement. To avoid double counting and ambiguity, the following conventions should be applied:

— Every tourism stay has only one corresponding origin of the trip, which is the actual place of residence of the visitor

— Every tourism trip can have several destinations but only one main destination;

— Every tourism trip has only one main purpose, which is the purpose in the absence of which the trip would not have taken place.

Destination: This is a significant place visited during a trip/stay. It may be defined as the farthest point away from home visited (distance destination), the place where the most amount of time is spent (main destination), or the place the visitor thinks of as the primary place visited (motivating destination).

Duration of a visit: The duration of a visit (stay or trip) is measured in the units of the number of hours for same-day visits, and of nights for staying visits. The duration is measured either in terms of time spent in the receiving place/country for inbound tourism (= Duration of the stay), or time away from the usual residence for outbound tourism (= Duration of the trip).

Main purpose of the visit: this is the purpose in the absence of which the trip would not have been made or the given destination would not have been visited.

Overnight visits: Short and long stays concern the activities of visitors who stay overnight in collective or private accommodation in the place (region, country) visited. An international tourist is an international visitor who stays at least one night in collective or private accommodation in the country visited. A domestic tourist refers to a domestic visitor who stays at least one night in collective or private accommodation in the place visited. An overnight stay may be defined differently depending on the statistical approach taken. From a destination-based perspective a person is counted as spending the night in a place visited only if the data of his/her arrival and departure are different. From an origin-based perspective a person spends a night on a qualifying trip if (a) the date of his departure and return are different, and (b) s/he sleeps in collective or private accommodation during his absence.

Same-day visits: Same-day visits concern the activities of visitors who do not stay overnight in collective or private accommodation in the place (region, country) visited. A same-day visitor is defined as a visitor who does not spend the night in collective or private accommodation in the place or country visited. An international same-day visitor is an international visitor who does not spend the night in collective or private accommodation in the place or country visited A domestic same-day visitor is a domestic visitor who does not spend the night in collective or private accommodation in the place visited The same criteria and delimitations as for visitors apply to same-day visitors.

To avoid ambiguity it is important to distinguish three types of same-days visits based on the place of departure and arrival:

- Round trips starting from the place of usual residence (and other places to which one is not a visitor)
- Round trips from a place at which one is an overnight visitor
- Stopovers as part of transit travel

Only visits of the first type, round trips starting from the place of usual residence, are classified as same-day visits from an origin-based as well as a destination-based perspective.

Visits of the second type are part of long/short overnight visits and will only be classified as a same-day visit from a destination-based perspective.

Visits of the third type differ from the other two types by the fact that the nights before and after the same-day visit are spent in different places, which are also different from where the transit stop takes place. They will only be classified as a same-day visit from a destination-based perspective.

To avoid double counting with overnight visits, data on the first type of same day visits should always be distinguished from the other two types.

The statistical unit to be measured in tourism demand surveys carried out in homes may be:

(i) A household whose tourism participation is reported by one respondent speaking for the visits made by all members of the household, or an individual selected randomly from within a household, responding only for him/herself, or an individual identified by quota controls set by an agency responsible for the conduct of a quota sample.

(ii) A visitors selected by a random or quota control procedure, or a travelling party, selected by a random or a quota control procedure. A travelling party is not necessarily the same as a household group.

The sampling for surveys in respondents' homes, as well as in destination surveys and at international arrival and departure points, should be of individuals aged 15 or over, selected at random or according to a quota control procedure. The tourism activity of children can be measured by asking the adults about the children's tourism habits.

Data on the volume of tourism:

(a) Estimates of the generation of tourism demand (percentage and characteristics of each country's population and number of people participating in tourism on one or more occasions).

(b) Estimates of the number of visits made by the population participating in tourism (domestic and outbound = national tourism).

(c) Estimates of the number of visits of non-residents received within a country (inbound visitors).

(d) Estimates of the number of visits generated by the residents of a country to other countries (outbound visitors).

Data on Visitor profile: Information on the visitor profile provides vital data for analysing the nature of tourism demand. It tells us who the visitors are, i.e. the personal characteristics of the visitor : sex, age, level of education, economic activity status, occupation, income, household composition. In order to analyse tourism demand (and its various market segments), it is important to link information on the personal characteristics of the visitor (profile) with information on the purpose, behaviour and habits of the visitor (characteristics of the visit).

Data on the characteristics of the trip, including purpose of visit: These data describe the trip itself and involve relating the variables to the classification of the purpose of the visit, duration of the stay, accommodation used, transport used, activities engaged in and destination types visited. They also cover the areas/destinations visited, months of departure and types of overall tourism product purchased - including use of packages/inclusive tours or independent travel.

Information on the purpose of the trip is useful in segmenting the tourism markets. In order to obtain a more accurate picture, it is useful to include the secondary purpose. Questions covering destination types, purpose of the visit and visitor activities are needed to calculate estimated participation in rural tourism, cultural or specific kinds of tourism markets.

The duration of the trip is a very important item of data : it is the most significant measure of the volume of the various tourism activities, such as accommodation; it is instrumental in establishing the maximum limit beyond which the trip is no longer considered to be part of tourism (one year); it distinguishes the tourist from the same-day visitor.

The means of transport has a strong bearing on visitor behaviour and expenditure. The mode of transport used refers to the mode used by the visitor to travel from his/her place of usual residence to the places visited. The main mode of transport used is defined as the conveyance used to cover the greatest distance. In many cases it is also interesting to know the secondary or other modes of transport which may have been used during the visit. Information on the distance covered to the destination and back is also a valuable variable, which can be linked to transport, energy and environment statistics. The classification breakdown of the distance covered may be finer for same-day visits than for short and long stays. Links with transport statistics on passenger mobility can provide useful information.

Data on tourism expenditure: Data on tourism expenditure form part of the processes involved in estimating the balance of payments and employment attributed to tourism. The approach may be different according to whether it is origin-based or destination based. In the first case, one would be interested in all the expenditures for the trip, including advance outlay necessary for the preparation and undertaking of the trip and travel-related outlays made in the place of residence after returning from the trip. From a destination-based perspective, the primary interest would be the expenditures made in the place visited. But this does not affect the variables or classifications as such.

Tourism expenditure in general and international tourism expenditure transactions are discussed in more detail in the chapter on tourism in the Balance of payments.

To optimise the total resources devoted to measuring tourism activity, information on demand and supply should be co-ordinated. The services and products in demand can be linked to the supply of these by studying tourism expenditure and activities. This presupposes that demand statistics are recorded in detail and that the statistics on supply are compiled according to the tourism demand classifications. Two important tourism-related statistics in this field are services statistics and the commodity accounting of input-output accounts.

For some key statistical variables in countries with registration requirements and some form of voluntary or legal enforcement, important aspects of tourism demand may be measured indirectly through the statistics on tourism accommodation:

— estimates of the total number of visitors staying in commercial accommodation in a country or a particular destination may be derived directly through guest registrations;

— if the regulations covering accommodation registration require visitors to complete registration forms, or if international transport data can be supplemented with limited data available from immigration/emigration cards, supply-side data may also be used to help estimate purpose of travel (business/holiday etc.), size of travelling party, and place of residence or origin of visitors. Such methods only produce valid results, however, where strict controls are applied to the data collection process.

Demand for a country or region may be partly estimated through an analysis of passenger transport data. In each of the cases above, however, for the data to meet identified user needs for demand purposes, it is necessary to know what proportion of all tourism uses the supply of products and services offered. Such proportions can only be derived from surveys of overall demand.

Tourism Supply

The definition of tourism supply should result from the definition of tourism. Thus it can be defined as the supply of all assets, services and goods to be enjoyed or bought by visitors and occasioned by the journeys of visitors. Statistics on tourism supply may be approached in two ways :

— statistics on the production (structure) of enterprises etc., e.g. supply has been interpreted as activities of enterprises such as the supply of HORECA, transport and retail services;

— statistics on the results of such activities, i.e. products, which also may be services, consumed by visitors;

The general purpose of statistics on tourism supply is to assess the contribution of the tourism sector to a country's general socio-economic process and to identify the effects of tourism, distinguishing between direct effects and indirect or induced effects.

Some economic activities depend on tourism for their survival, e.g. tourist accommodation, travel agencies, long-distance passenger transport. Other activities such as restaurants and bars, car rental services, entertainment and attractions services also tend to rely strongly on tourism. The dependency of certain activities of enterprises on tourism may also depend on their location. Thus the supply of tourism activities comprises diverse economic activities, and presented as a sector is very heterogeneous, encompassing different activities some of which are directly dependent on tourism and others only partly.

To delimit and define in more detail tourism activities, the WTO has drawn up the International Standard Classification of Tourism Activities : SICTA. This classification was adopted by the Statistical Division of the United Nations and is based on the revised International Standard Industrial classification. SICTA remains at present a provisional classification. It attempts to distinguish between activities which receive their revenue primarily from tourism (labelled "T") and activities which have a partial relationship with tourism (labelled "P").

Many types of data can be observed from the activities of enterprises (production units) :

— Data on the unit itself, such as type of activity, size, legal status

— Data on the production factors, such as breakdown of fixed assets, labour

— Accounting data, such as the breakdown of turnover or value added

— Data on the output (goods and services) of the unit, expressed in physical quantities and distinguished according to the nature of the product and use of the production capacity

— Data on the prices and tariffs of goods and services sold.

Institutional statistics on the sectors of activities related to tourism generally fall within the framework of Enterprise statistics, so that direct reference can be made to other parts of the Eurostat Manual of Business Statistics, developed by the Statistical Office of the European Communities.

Supply of tourism products

The global product approach deals not only with products as direct results of economic activities but all products (diversions, goods and services) that are enjoyed or bought by visitors.

Tourism products may be considered as follows:

— Products (goods and services) consumed by visitors that can be described by a standard product classification such as the Central Product classification by Activities (CPA) or the CPC (Central Product Classification);

— natural assets of a location, such as mountains, beaches, lakes, etc. and weather conditions, the environment in general;

— attitude of the population to visitors, the lifestyle and culture of the receiving area

The products supplied represent more than tourism expenditure. Tourism expenditure is the counterpart of the majority of products having the shape of goods and services, although not every good or service has to be paid for by the consumer.

The use of assets (e.g. roads, historical areas, national park, nature) in many cases is free, in other cases visitors have to pay for the facility offered (a 'service'). In fact, most assets offer 'services' to their users or to the people enjoying them, regardless of whether visitors have to pay for them or not. Nevertheless, free 'services' of the type which benefit from the infrastructure of a country belong to the supply of tourism products. Free for the visitor does not mean that the free service is also free for the supplier ; the country has to spend money in order to maintain fresh air, etc. Because these types of products are hard to quantify, they are excluded from the statistical analysis.

To make the definition of the supply of tourism products practical, only products which can be identified in a standard product classification are taken into account. In defining the supply of tourism products, two considerations (representing two sides of the same coin) must be kept in mind:

— the supply of tourism products includes all products supplied to the visitor, including non-characteristic tourism products.

— products that are consumed by visitors may also be consumed by other types of consumer.

Therefore, when attempting to measure the supply of tourism products, one must attempt to identify the share of the product which is consumed by visitors.

The reporting unit that can best supply information about the product under review depends on the type of product to be observed. In general the following may be used as a reporting unit: enterprise, local unit, kind-of-activity-unit (KAU), local KAU, (local authorities) of a community, province etc. Since the observation unit is the product, the reporting unit should be asked to provide information on the breakdown of their activities according to kind-of-activity units or supply the breakdown by sales of products.

As tourism is basically a demand-oriented concept, the need to collect information from the demand side is essential in order to know the destination of goods and services produced and therefore complete the supply-side data. The demand of residents can be estimated by demand-side statistics, the total tourism demand within a certain country can be estimated via supply-side statistics. By deducting demand of residents from total demand, the non resident tourism demand may be calculated.

Administrative data such as registers of enterprises and establishments maintained by the tax authorities, registers of establishments prepared by the CSOs, register of establishments maintained by health or licensing authorities, can be used to identify production units supplying tourism products and to obtain basic information on the production unit. In many cases, information relating to tourism products can be obtained directly from enterprises or other statistical units. Information on some types of facilities may be gathered through accommodation statistics. Information on certain tourism products may be derived from enterprise, transport, consumption statistics and statistics on prices.

Tourism Accommodation Statistics

A large share of short-term accommodation supply is taken up by tourists. The basic aim of tourism accommodation statistics is to measure the capacity and use of collective accommodation establishments and (if possible) of private means of accommodation. Tourist accommodation is defined as: "any facility that regularly provides overnight accommodation for tourists". It is important to distinguish facilities that commercially service the bulk of overnight stays away from the guest's usual environment and those providing occasional overnight accommodation. Thus tourist accommodation has been divided into two main groups:

- collective accommodation establishments and
- private tourist accommodation.

Collective tourist accommodation

Collective tourist accommodation is defined as an accommodation establishment providing overnight lodging for the traveller in a room or some other unit, but the number of places it provides must be greater than a specified minimum for groups of persons exceeding a single family unit and all the places in the establishment must come under a common commercial-type management, even if it is not for profit.

The major group "collective tourist accommodation establishment" is subdivided into three minor groups:

hotels and similar establishments, specialised establishments, and other collective establishments. These minor groups are further subdivided into nine unit groups.

Hotels or similar establishments: This category is typified as being arranged in rooms, in number exceeding a specified minimum; as coming together under a common management; as providing certain services including room services and daily bed-making and cleaning of the sanitary facilities; as grouped in classes and categories according to the facilities and services provided; and as not falling in the category of a specialised establishments.

— *Hotels*: Comprises hotels, apartment-hotels, motels, roadside inns, beach hotels and similar establishments providing hotel services, including more than daily bed-making and cleaning of the rooms and sanitary facilities.

— *Similar establishments*: Comprises rooming and boarding houses, bed-and-breakfast establishments, tourist residences and similar accommodation arranged in rooms and providing limited hotel services, including daily bed-making and cleaning of the rooms and sanitary facilities.

Specialised establishments: This category is typified as being any establishment intended for tourists, which may be non-profit making; as coming under a common management; as providing minimum common services (not including daily bed-making); as not necessarily being arranged in rooms but perhaps in dwelling-type units, camp sites or collective dormitories; and as engaging in some activity besides the provision of accommodation, such as health care, social welfare, conferences or transport. This minor group consists of establishments that, besides providing accommodation, have another specialised function. This minor group is subdivided into four unit groups : health establishments, work and holiday camps, conference centres and accommodation in collective means of transport, which are described as follows :

— *Health establishments*: This unit group comprises health treatment and health care establishments providing accommodation, such as spas, thermal resorts, (mountain) sanatoria, convalescent homes, health farms, fitness resorts and other similar establishments.

— *Work and holiday camps*: This unit group comprises camps providing accommodation for holiday activities, such as agricultural, archaeological and ecological work camps, holiday camps, scout camps, riding and sailing schools, other sports centres, and other similar establishments.

— *Passenger transport*: This unit group consists of the accommodation with sleeping facilities associated with collective public transport and inseparable from it in terms or fare. It comprises cruise ships of all kinds (usually not using marinas to stay overnight), accommodation in scheduled passenger ships and sleeping-car and couchette accommodation in trains and motor coaches, and other accommodation in public or hired means of transport . This is a special category of accommodation in the sense that it is mobile.

— *Conference centres*: This unit group includes establishments offering accommodation and specialised in facilities for congresses, conferences, courses, vocational training, meditation, retreats, etc. The sleeping accommodation is generally only available to the participants of the specialised activities organised in or by the establishment.

Other collective establishments: This category is typified as being any establishment intended for holiday-makers, which may be non-profit making; as coming under a common management; as providing minimum common services (not including daily bed-making); and as not necessarily being arranged in rooms but perhaps in dwelling-type units, camp sites or collective dormitories. This minor group consists of establishments arranged as holiday dwellings, tourist campsites and social tourism accommodation.

— *Holiday dwellings:* This unit group includes collective facilities under common management, such as apartment buildings, clusters of houses or bungalows arranged as dwelling-type accommodation. Often tourist services such as recreational activities, canteen, laundry facilities and information services are provided.

— *Tourist campsites*: This unit group consists of collective facilities in enclosed areas for tents, caravans, trailers and mobile homes. All come under common management and provide some tourism services (shop, information, recreational activities, canteen, laundry facilities).

— *Other collective establishments*: This unit group comprises social and group tourist accommodation establishments and marinas. Social tourist accommodation includes youth hostels, tourist dormitories, group accommodation, holiday homes for the elderly, holiday accommodation for employees and workers' hotels, halls of residence for students and school dormitories and other similar facilities that come under common management, have a social interest and are often subsidised. Marinas are also included under this unit group. Marinas include boating harbours where boat owners can hire a permanent berth in the water or a place on the land for the sailing season or the year (long-term hire) and ports for passing vessels where sailors pay mooring per nights. At least some sanitary facilities are provided.

Private tourist accommodation

Private tourist accommodation comprises forms of accommodation that do not conform to the definition of collective tourist accommodation. These provide limited numbers of places for rent or free of charge. The major group "Private tourism accommodation" is subdivided into two minor groups and five unit groups. It is important to distinguish between the minor group "private rental accommodation" and "private non-rental accommodation", as the former generates lodging expenditures and an associated economic impact that the latter does not.

Private rental accommodation

— Rented rooms in family houses: The accommodation covered by this unit group differs from the boarding house in that the tourist stays with the family that usually lives in the home and pays rent.

— Dwellings rented from private individuals or professional agencies: This unit group comprises apartments, villas, houses, chalets and other dwellings rented or leased as complete units between households, on a temporary basis, as tourist accommodation.

Private non-rental accommodation: This minor group concerns lodging places offered free of charge to guests.

— *Owned dwelling*: This unit group comprises immobile units such as second homes/apartments, villas, houses, chalets, and other dwellings used by visitors who are members of the owner household. This group also includes dwellings incorporated in a time-sharing contract (owned by various people).

— *Accommodation provided without charge by relatives or friends*: The accommodation of this unit concerns tourists allowed by relatives or friends to use all or part of their home free of charge.

Other private accommodation: his unit group does not fit entirely into the major group of private tourist accommodation. It includes other types of accommodation such as tents, caravans, trailers, campers at non-organised sites (not placed in collective tourism accommodation) and vessels at unofficial moorings.

Because regional aspects and characteristics of the accommodation establishment itself are very important to the results of accommodation statistics, local kind-of-activity units (KAU) should be used as the basic statistical unit, e.g. the observation unit in accommodation statistics. Alternatively the local unit can be used as the basic statistical unit of tourism accommodation establishments. In some cases the enterprise and the local unit coincide, but it is quite common for one enterprise to comprise two or more establishments or facilities of the same kind or of a different kind. This is one reason why the tourism accommodation establishments classification used for tourism statistics described on the previous pages does not have a one-to-one relationship with activity or product classifications.

The supply and capacity of tourist accommodation concerns information on the number of establishments providing their services to tourists, and on the structure and quality of this supply. The use of tourist accommodation concerns information on guest flows.

Variables on the supply and capacity of tourist accommodation establishments:

(i) Number of establishments according to each type of accommodation

(ii) Overnight capacity, number of:

a) *Bed-places*: The number of bed-places in an establishment or dwelling is determined by the number of persons who can stay overnight in beds set up in the establishments, ignoring any extra beds that may be set up by customer request. The term bed-place applies to a single bed. A double bed is counted as two bed-places. This unit serves to measure the capacity of any type of accommodation. A bed-place is also a pitch or, in a boat, a mooring to accommodate one person. A pitch for a tent (if counted), caravan, mobile home and similar shelter, or a boat on a mooring, usually counts for 4 bed-places if the actual number is not known.

b) *Bedrooms*: A bedroom is a unit formed by one room or groups of rooms constituting an indivisible rental whole in an accommodation establishment or dwelling. Rooms may be single, double or multiple, depending on whether they are equipped permanently to sleep one, two or several people. The number of existing rooms is the number the establishment habitually has available to accommodate guests (tourists). If a room is used as a permanent residence (for more than one year) it should not be included. Bathrooms and toilets do not count as a room. This number should generally coincide with the number of units recorded in the establishment recorder. Apartments are a special type of room. They consist of one or more rooms and have a kitchen unit and own bathroom and toilet. Apartments may be with or without hotel services. Cabins, cottages, huts, chalets, bungalows, villas and summerhouses can be treated like bedrooms and apartments, i.e. to be let as a single unit.

c) *Pitch and mooring*: The majority of camp sites let pitches for tents, caravans, mobile homes and similar shelter to tourists who want to stay on a 'touring' pitch for only a couple of consecutive days or weeks, as well as to people who want to hire a 'fixed' pitch for a season or a year. Moorings on boats in marinas can be dealt with similarly to pitches. Hired fixed pitches and moorings for long-term rent (more than a year) may also be considered as private accommodation. It is advisable to obtain monthly data on the number of bed-places, bedrooms, pitches and moorings because they may change according to the season and are needed in order to calculate occupancy rates.

(iii) Months (or days) open during the year: This variable is necessary to get an impression of the seasonal aspects of the business, and to calculate the occupancy rates.

(iv) Services offered - Number of establishments offering: a) Restaurant services is the most important variable of services offered. Other variables may be: b)breakfast (buffet/other), c)lunch, d)dinner, e)bar services (only for staying guests / for other clients also), f) M2 conference rooms, g) swimming pool, h) sauna or solarium, i) sports facilities, j) (other) facilities for health treatment, k) shops, l) children's playgrounds / play room, m) laundry service, n) self-service laundry, o) self-catering kitchen, p) guarded or closed parking, q) amusement (e.g. dancing).

(v) Other quality criteria - Number of establishments with: a) Awarded quality classifications, e.g. stars, crowns, flags, etc. b) Bathrooms for individual use c) (Bedrooms) provided with heating and suitable for all-year accommodation. Other variables may be d) soundproof rooms, e) rooms provided with air conditioning, f) length of the majority of the beds, g) rooms with audio equipment and television.

(i) *Guest flows* - Numbers of arrivals and overnight stays:

a) Arrivals (or departures) of accommodation establishment guests

— by country of residence of the guest

— by month

A guest arrival/departure is defined as a person

who arrives at/leaves a collective accommodation establishment or private tourism accommodation and checks in/out.

Because tourists arrive at and leave from an accommodation establishment within a relatively short time, there is statistically not much difference between the numbers of arrivals and departures. The arrivals of non-tourists (refugees, guests on medical referral, etc.) should be counted separately, if possible.

b) Overnight stays of accommodation establishment guests

— by country of residence of the guest

— by month

An overnight stay (or night spent) is each night that a traveller stays or is registered in a collective accommodation establishment or in private tourism accommodation, his or her physical presence there being unnecessary.

The overnights stays of non-tourists should be counted separately if possible.

(ii) *Average length of stay*: This variable is obtained by dividing the number of overnight stays by the number of arrivals (can calculate also according to country of residence of guests). It is more relevant at local and regional level because at country level, the effect of same persons spending nights in several places obscures the measurement.

(iii) *Purpose of the visit*: This can be counted either by number of guests or overnight stays.

(iv) *Variables on occupancy*: Occupancy rates give information on differences in use between various types of accommodation and, when measured on a monthly basis, indicate the seasonal patterns.

a) *Net occupancy rate of bed-places*: The net occupancy rate of bed-places in one month is obtained by dividing total overnight stays by the product of bed-places on offer and the number of days when the bed-places are actually available for use (net of seasonal or other temporary closures for decoration, police order, etc.) for the same group of establishments, multiplying the quotient by 100 to express the result as a percentage.

b) *Gross occupancy rate of bed-rooms*: The gross occupancy rate of bed-places in one month is obtained by dividing total overnight stays by the product of bed-places on offer and the number of days in the corresponding month (sometimes termed bed-nights) for the same group of establishments, multiplying the quotient by 100 to express the result as a percentage.

c) *Net occupancy rate of rooms (houses, pitches, moorings)*: For hotels and similar establishments, the room occupancy rate can be a better measure of capacity utilisation than bed occupancy because a room with a double bed is very often occupied by only one person. This is calculated by dividing the total number of rooms used during the month (the sum of the rooms in use per day) by the average number of rooms available for the month multiplying the quotient by 100 to express the result as a percentage.

d) *Gross occupancy rate of rooms (houses, pitches, moorings)*: This can be calculated in the same way as for bed-places.

Accommodation statistics figure partially as a second-best alternative to gain information on the demand side of tourism, especially on tourists from abroad. Results of accommodation statistics provide information on the use of accommodation, as well as on some variables of some categories of tourists (i.e. purpose of visit). In this way they give information on demand. Accommodation statistics data in one country provide additional information to demand-side tourism data of another country.

A solid connection can be found between accommodation statistics and services statistics on the horeca sector. Generally, accommodation statistics are census-based and services statistics are sample-based, but if both use the same address register, it is then possible to connect data on an individual basis and to interpret financial data on tourism. Important variables such as the proprietorship of the establishment, the number of persons employed, and general monetary variables can be obtained from business registers, services statistics, labour force surveys.

An updated register of names and addresses of accommodation establishments is extremely important. Guidebooks and tourism organisations are good sources of capacity, services offered and quality classifications. For commercial private accommodation, the intermediary agencies are an important source. For non-commercial private accommodation, housing registers, censuses and surveys may give information, e.g. the number of second homes.

As there is a strong interest in regional data, most European countries have census surveys for tourist establishments. For larger countries it is possible to use samples without losing much reliability at country level.Countries use different legal or statistical standards for excluding minimal-capacity tourist accommodation suppliers. The threshold is usually based on the number of rooms, (or pitches) or beds. The threshold chosen should be determined in such a way that at least 95% of all nights spent in the groups of accommodation establishments included in accommodation statistics are covered.

On some countries there are legal obligations for the guests to give information to the establishment. If there is no legal act that requires tourist to fill in registration forms, information can be obtained on a voluntary basis, or simply from the night registers of the establishment. In some countries businesses are required to fill out and send the questionnaires of accommodation statistics to the national statistical authority. When the replies are checked regularly and reminders sent to the establishments failing to send the data on time, high response rates are possible.

Tourism Expenditure

Tourism expenditure is defined as "the total consumption expenditure made by a visitor, or on behalf of a visitor, for and during his/her trip and stay at destination". This concept encompasses a wide variety of items, ranging from the purchase of consumer goods and services inherent in travel and stays to the purchase of small durable goods for personal use, souvenirs and gifts for family and friends. Tourism expenditure is not restricted to payments made during the visit. It also includes advance outlays necessary for the preparation and undertaking of the trip and travel-related purchases made in the place of residence after returning from a trip. These categories refer to payments for travel insurance, transport, the purchase of travel guides, etc.

There are certain types of outlays or acquisitions which are to be excluded from tourism expenditure. These are purchases for commercial purposes, capital-type investments or transactions (e.g., real estate, cars, boats, etc..), even if they may in the future be used for tourism purposes, and cash or donations made to private persons or institutions which do not represent payment for tourism goods or services.

Total tourism expenditure can be broken down from different perspectives :

— Domestic and international tourism expenditure;

— Within international expenditure, between transport fares and other types of expenditure;

— Expenditures on same-day visits and overnight stays;

— The products to which the expenditures relates.

Domestic tourism expenditures are defined as expenditures incurred as a direct result of resident visitors travelling within their own country of residence.

International tourism expenditures are defined as expenditures of outbound visitors in other countries, including their payments to foreign carriers for international transport (although for the sake of consistency with the Balance of Payments recommendations of the International Monetary Fund

(IMF) it is recommended to classify these international fare expenditures separately). They should also include any other prepayments or payments made afterwards for goods and services purchased from the countries visited.

International fare expenditures are defined as all payments made to carriers registered abroad by any person resident in the compiling country.

International tourism receipts are defined as expenditures of international inbound visitors, including their payments to national carriers for international transport (although for the sake of consistency with the Balance of Payments recommendations of the International Monetary Fund (IMF) it is recommended to classify these international fare receipts separately). They should include any other prepayments or payments made afterwards for goods and services purchased from the country visited.

International fare receipts are defined as all payments made to the carriers registered in the compiling country of sums owed by non-resident visitors, whether or not they are travelling in that country.

Tourism in the Balance of payments

Tourism expenditure in the Balance of Payments concerns international tourism expenditure. Expenditures by outbound travellers are generally a debit of the given country, while expenditures by inbound travellers in the country constitute a credit. The Balance of Payments includes tourism expenditure of international visitors (tourists and same-day visitors) within a defined accounting scheme with its own methodology established in the International Monetary Fund (IMF) Balance of

Payments manual. In these recommendations, international tourism expenditure is covered by 2 items:

— Travel

— Other transportation, passenger services,

All tourist expenditures, except international fare payments (which is under passenger services) are included under the Travel item.

There are three basic concepts to be considered in international tourism expenditure: residence, visitor and tourism expenditure, since only the expenditure of resident visitors travelling abroad and that of non-resident visitors travelling to the compiling economy is to be taken into account.

Tourism statistics attempt to remain as consistent as possible with the IMF Balance of Payments recommendations. However, the IMF definition of its "Travel" item, i.e. the expenditure of international "travellers" is broader than that of the definition of tourism and the "visitor" in tourism statistics. This leads to two major discrepancies between what is included in the Travel item of the Balance of Payments and what is included in international tourism expenditure from the conceptual approach of tourism statistics :

— The IMF considers students and medical patients as residents of their economy of origin, even if their length of stay is over one year, and therefore includes their expenditure under "Travel". By contrast, such travellers are excluded from the visitor concept in tourism statistics because their length of stay exceeds one consecutive year, and their expenditures are therefore excluded from international tourism expenditure.

— The IMF includes expenditure of seasonal and border workers under "Travel". By contrast, the definition of the visitor in tourism statistics excludes seasonal and border workers because their main purpose is the exercise of an activity remunerated from within the place visited, and their expenditures are therefore excluded from international tourism expenditure.

From the Balance of Payments perspective, the Statistical unit to be considered differs according to the system used. For the Balance of Payments two broad approaches are used to measure travel expenditure:

(i) *The International Transaction Reporting System (ITRS).* This approach attempts to measure the instruments used to pay for the travel. It compiles information for the Balance of Payments on receipts and payments between resident and non-residents. In principle, in systems based on international receipts and payments data, the statistical unit is either the resident travelling abroad or the resident enterprise that pays non-residents for services to be provided to residents travelling abroad or is paid by non-residents for services provided during their stay in the country. Usually, this information is reported to the compiling organisation through the credit institutions (banks, savings banks, etc.) that effect their receipts and payments. In turn, these credit institutions report their transactions with foreign-currency notes and coin and the notes and coin of their own country surrendered to non-resident credit institutions.

(ii) *Enterprise surveys (ES) and additional surveys relating directly to visitors and their expenditure.* Enterprise surveys concern the collection of information on international transactions undertaken by resident enterprises. Such supply-or demand-side surveys attempt to measure the actual expenditure by travellers. In systems based on supply-side surveys, the statistical reporting unit is defined in "Statistical units" of Tourism Supply, i.e. the enterprise, local unit, etc. In systems based on demand-side surveys, the statistical reporting unit is defined in "Statistical units" of Tourism Demand, i.e. a household or individual in household surveys and a visitor or travelling party in surveys at international arrival and departure points or destinations.

To date there has not been a very close connection between international receipts and payments from the Balance of payments and tourism supply and demand statistics. A closer relationship between data obtained from the regular registration of exchange transactions by central banks and data obtained from surveys on tourism, and even the use of the latter to estimate, compare and check the former, would improve the overall quality of the data on international tourism expenditure. To improve the results, the following actions are recommended:

Short-term action

— Exchange of information between the various countries on both "Passenger transport" and bank note transactions on a uniform basis and use at EEA level.

— Unification of estimate and adjustment criteria.

— Increased use of tourism and transport statistics to check data quality or as a source for estimates and adjustments.

Long-term action

With the introduction of a common European currency in the near future, it will be impossible to obtain information on cash receipts and payments made between EU Member states, so that it is advisable in the future to replace the current data collection systems by other methods. In principle, the most obvious way seems to be to obtain information on Balance of Payments debits through household surveys. The exchange of information between EU Member States would provide each Member State with credit data in a similar way as between the United States and Canada. The remaining credits could be estimated through visitor surveys or other estimates, and information could also be exchanged with some other countries using a system similar to the one applied at EU level.

Tourism prices, costs and tariffs

Prices on tourism can be considered as:

— prices (including tariffs) of goods and services linked to tourism, the level of which influence tourism expenditure. The prices of these goods and services are related to the demand side of tourism and are consumer prices;

— prices of goods and services which determine the cost of tourism production. The prices of these goods and services refer to the supply side of tourism and are called either cost of production prices or input prices on tourism.

The level of prices paid by visitors is influenced by tourism demand. Increasing demand for goods and services related to tourism will have an impact on their prices. On the other hand, the level of prices of goods and services related to tourism affects tourism demand.

Prices related to goods and services of intermediate consumption for tourism activities, the remuneration of the factors of tourism production and the prices for goods and services contributing to fixed capital formation on tourism sector affect the cost of tourism supply. Although in many cases the real prices and changes are interesting to measure, this section will focus on price changes measured by constructing price indices which combine the different changes in prices of individual items in such a way that a single number can be used to indicate the overall change in prices.

The main variable considered here is Prices indices, and as such can be included as an economic variable for the tourism sector.

Price indices on tourism can be divided into the following two main categories:

(i) price indices from the demand side (consumer prices);

(ii) price indices from the supply side (cost of production).

Price indices on tourism from the demand side measure changes in prices over time of a given pattern of tourism expenditure, or compare the price level of tourism expenditure in space. Therefore, these indices can be subdivided into:

(a) inter-temporal (time) price indices, and

(b) inter-spatial (space) price indices.

Many inter-temporal price indices from the demand side can be constructed depending on the expenditure covered by each index. The inter-spatial price indices can be distinguished into:

— inter-regional price indices, which make comparisons of the price level of tourism expenditure between regions of a country, and

— international price indices, which compare the price level of tourism expenditure between countries.

A "Tourism Expenditure Price Index" can measure the price changes of total expenditure made by all visitors (residents and non-residents) in the economic territory of a country (region, area). Tourism price indices from the supply side measure changes over time of the cost of producing tourism products. The measurement of the changes in the cost of production for the tourism sector as a whole or by activity can be achieved by measuring changes in prices of the main cost elements. The main cost elements are:

— Intermediate consumption, which represents the value of the goods and market services consumed by production units during the course of the relevant period in order to produce goods and services related to tourism;

— Remuneration of factors of production;

— Depreciation of fixed capital. The measurement of the changes in this cost element is achieved indirectly by measuring the changes in prices of goods and services contributing to fixed capital formation.

Consequently, the following price indices from the supply side can be constructed :

(i) price indices of intermediate consumption, which measure over time changes in prices of a given pattern of intermediate consumption of production units engaged in tourism activities;

(ii) price indices of fixed capital formation, which measure over time the changes in prices of goods and services contributing to capital formation in tourism activities.

(iii) price indices of the production factors, which measure over time changes in the remuneration of factors of production engaged in tourism activities.

Tourism expenditure price statistics (demand side) refer to the prices of goods and services consumed by visitors. The consumption of visitors is a part of the final consumption of households. Many goods and services consumed by visitors are also consumed by non-visitors. All goods and services of households' final consumption are therefore to be carefully combined with the activity classification, following which products and services which are exclusively or partially consumed by visitors are to be identified.

Tourism price statistics from the supply side (costs and their price indices) will be calculated for activities which are mainly or partly dependent on tourism. The goods and services which constitute the intermediate consumption of each tourism activity, as well as the goods and services contributing to the fixed capital formation, will be classified according to the activity branches of the whole economy from which they come.

Tourism price indices from the demand side are closely linked with statistics on tourism expenditure. The results of tourism expenditure surveys, broken down by categories according to the visitors' place of residence (residents, non-residents) and purpose of travelling as well as by type of expenditure, are necessary for the calculation of the weighting scheme of tourism price indices from the demand side.

Surveys of tourism expenditure are usually conducted at rather long intervals (three or more years), and the estimation of tourism expenditure for the intermediate years is therefore achieved by using extrapolation methods based on time tourism price indices. The purpose of time tourism price indices from the demand side is to measure the changes over time in tourism expenditure due to price changes. Consequently, tourism expenditure and tourism price indices are interconnected variables. Comparisons in real terms of tourism expenditure between countries is achieved by using the space price indices from the demand side. The price level and its changes, measured by price indices, influence tourism demand. Additionally, the differences in real terms of price level between countries, measured by space price indices, influence tourism demand of the countries because these differences determine their competitive position.

Tourism price indices from the supply side are linked with surveys on enterprises, from which (surveys) cost production data (intermediate consumption, remuneration of the factors of production) as well as data referring to fixed capital formation can be derived. The results of surveys on the cost by activity are necessary for the estimation of the weights of the corresponding price indices. Moreover, as the above surveys are probably not conducted every year, the price indices are useful for estimation of the changes in several cost elements due to price changes, for the intermediate years. Finally, regardless of the periodicity of the costs surveys, the price indices from the supply side of tourism can be used for measuring the effect of price changes on the cost of production. Consequently, costs and price indices on tourism from the supply side are mutually connected.

Link with other statistics:

(i) Tourism price indices from the demand side are linked with the following statistics:

(a) Consumer Price Index refers to the prices of goods and services of households' consumption, a part of which is the consumption of resident visitors. Therefore, some goods and services included in the Consumer Price Index are related to tourism consumption, and their price indices can be used in the calculation of the Tourism Expenditure Price Index.

(b) Family Budget Surveys cover all the expenses of households, some of which are related to the expenditure of resident visitors.

(c) Survey of Purchasing Power Parities covers, among other things, private consumption, part of which refers to tourism consumption. Consequently, it includes some goods and services linked to tourism, the prices of which can be used in the calculation of international space price indices on tourism.

(ii) Tourism price indices from the supply side are linked with the following statistics:

(a) Input-Output tables, from which useful data concerning flows on tourism activities can be obtained and used in the estimation of the weights of the corresponding price indices.

(b) National Accounts can be taken into account especially for the index of gross fixed capital formation on tourism.

(c) Wholesale Price Indices. Some goods included in these indices refer to intermediate consumption or to gross fixed capital formation on tourism, and their price indices can be used for the calculation of the corresponding price indices on tourism.

(d) Construction Price Indices. Some constructions (buildings, public works etc.) refer to tourism, and the relevant individual price indices can be used in the calculation of Gross Fixed Capital Formation Indices on Tourism.

(e) Surveys on wages and salaries, provided they cover the tourism sector.

Guidelines for collection

— *Periodicity*: It is recommended that tourism price indices from both the demand and supply sides be calculated for at least every quarter of a year, in order to show the seasonal fluctuations of prices and rates, which are very strong in tourism.

— *Base period*: price indices are relative numbers obtained from comparison of prices of the present or current period with the corresponding prices of a previous period, which is called base period. A calendar year is proposed as a base period because the formulated prices within a period of one year are usually free of seasonal variations. To be able to compare prices between countries, a common base year has to be used.

The selection of items : this will be done from within each class or sub-class of the classification system used, and will be based on the following criteria :

(i) the economic importance of each item in relation to the class to which it belongs;

(ii) its quantitative and qualitative stability over time, and;

(iii) the representativeness of the selected items against the total items belonging to a given class.

Calculation of indices : from a practical point of view, it is recommended to use the Laspeyres formula, because it does not require the continuous recalculation of the weights, a procedure which is very difficult and expensive. The Laspeyres formula can be expressed as a weighted aggregate index or as a weighted mean of price relatives between the base period and the period under consideration.

Revision policy of indices : the weights and the composition of price indices calculated by using the Laspeyres formula are kept constant until the revision of the indices. Taking into consideration the nature of these indices, a five years revision is regarded as sufficient.

The Tourism Expenditure Price Index will cover all expenses made by all visitors (residents and non-residents) in the economic territory of a country (region, area). The structure of tourism expenditure, reflecting the relative importance of individual goods and services or groups of them within total or average tourism expenditure, can be analysed using information obtained from tourism demand surveys on expenditure. The weighting pattern provides the multipliers by which the prices, or price relatives, are combined for the calculation of the index. Combining data from various statistical sources, such as household budget surveys (expenditure data on residents), balance of payments (receipts from Inbound tourism), input-output tables, and tourism statistics on the volume of tourism (e.g. number of visitors, number of nights spent in tourist accommodation), may also give an estimation of the index weights.

The item sample is formed by the array of specific products, selected from among the entire range of tourism consumption items, for which prices are to be collected. The selected items have to be specified, so that changes in prices due to the change of quality, quantity and other characteristics are avoided.

The first stage of organising the price collection is the area selection for outlet sampling. The sample of outlets is to be drawn from many technical factors governing the selection of regions. In addition to the technical factors, the available resources are taken into account for the final decision of region selection. Once the representative regions have been selected, the problem of drawing a representative sample of price reporters is posed. An important factor in selecting the outlets is the correspondence that should exist between the outlet sample and visitor population covered by the index. It must be noted that in some cases prices or price relatives or indices of individual products can be obtained directly from the consumer prices index.

International price indices on tourism, which compare the price level of tourism expenditure between countries, are more complicated to calculate than inter-temporal price indices because of the need to maintain transitivity in multilateral price comparisons. It is therefore recommended to refer to the methodology developed by the Statistical Office of the European Communities in the field of Price statistics and to the survey of prices of household consumer goods and services. Some goods and services of this survey are linked to tourism, and their prices can be used directly for the construction of price indices comparing tourism expenditure between countries. Based on the existing methodology an International Price Level Index of Tourism Expenditure can be developed by covering the same expenditure items as for Tourism Expenditure Price Index.

Tourism price indices from the supply side, or "cost production indices on tourism", refer to the changes over time in tourism production cost due to prices changes.

The methodology used to construct the three categories of prices indices (intermediate consumption, production factors, fixed capital formation) is basically the same. The construction of price indices on the production factors should focus on "labour" and "capital".

The price indices of intermediate consumption will cover the value of the goods (other than capital goods) and market services consumed by producer units during the course of a period in order to produce other goods and services related to tourism. The price indices of factors of production will cover the total amount of compensation of employees engaged in tourism-related activities for the factor "Labour" and the actual interest of capital for the factor "Capital". The prices indices of fixed capital formation will cover the value of durable goods which are acquired by resident production units related to tourism in order to be used for a period of more than one year in the process of producing tourism products.

The weighting coefficients of the indices can be examined through specific surveys or studies which will combine existing data from several statistical sources on the supply of tourism activities. The values needed to calculate the weights for the intermediate consumption and capital formation indices must be free of deductible VAT. The selection of items of the indices will be made within each class or sub-class of the activity classification system.

Employment in Tourism

The tourism sector is very heterogeneous and encompasses many sectors of economic activity, which are either mainly (primary tourism activities), partly (secondary tourism activities) or indirectly (intermediary activities) dependent on tourism. When attempting to measure employment in tourism, one must first determine which sectors of activity will be taken into account. Employment can be measured in different ways according to the type of unit chosen. Two types of evaluation are possible:

Evaluation by observation:

a) *Activity-related evaluation:* measurement of employment in activities producing goods and services mainly or partly related to tourism.

b) *Labour force evaluation*: measurement of the labour force employed in activities mainly or partly related to tourism.

Model type evaluation

c) *Expenditure evaluation:* evaluation of the employment needed to produce goods and services consumed by visitors.

The three different types of analysis of tourism employment should be considered as complementary approaches, as each of them analyses the same topic from a different angle (e.g. regional aspects of tourism employment, working conditions, seasonality, etc.)

a) *Activity-related evaluation*: The simplest way to derive employment is to count the number of persons employed in sectors that deliver directly (without an intermediary) to the consumers of tourism goods and services. Since even for primary activities related to tourism, some service sectors not only have visitors as consumers but also local residents, the tourism-related employment can then be analysed through surveys carried out on the various types of clients and the respective services rendered. To be operational and practical, employment of the sector whose primary activity is tourism-related should be fully counted as tourism employment.

   A characteristic of the tourism supply sector is that it combines many small businesses which often cannot be taken into account in the general enterprise census. If a production evaluation approach is chosen for tourism employment statistics, the sample size must be enlarged, or stratified samples must be used. For producers whose second activity is tourism-related, surveys must be carried out in order to estimate the number of services bought by visitors and to calculate the resulting employment.

b) *Labour force evaluation*: It is rather difficult for an employee to decide if the product of his activity is sold or not to visitors. It is, however, possible for the persons surveyed to give information on the quota of visitors among their customers, and this, in combination with information gathered on the producer side, could help to define the tourism-related share of the business.

Tourism is characterised by its highly seasonal character. Tourism employment statistics must therefore take this aspect into consideration, and labour force surveys usually carried out at the end of every quarter should be organised separately at a more appropriate time for the tourism sector.

A major variable for tourism employment is the qualifications level of the persons employed which can be gathered from the labour force itself.

c) *Expenditure evaluation*: The person who knows best which goods were bought and which services were used is the visitor. The visitor or the final consumer must therefore be considered as the starting point of the analysis. From tourism expenditure surveys it is possible to derive information on the structure of consumption, although it varies depending on the destination of the trip, the purpose of the visit, the mode of transport and accommodation chosen, the number of people travelling together (especially for transport costs) and the month of the year. It is therefore important to take into account both the frequency of data collection and seasonal variations. Information on the selling point of goods and services is also needed, as many can be bought in different economic branches. The present expenditure surveys must be enlarged and carried out not only in the home base but also in places where visitors stay during their visits.

Calculation of the total consumption per sector by visitor is possible through the expenditure surveys.

The total labour force being known through other surveys, the "labour coefficient" (average labour unit per monetary consumption) can then be calculated. Knowing the number of labour units necessary for a certain monetary unit spent by visitors in a given sector, the direct employment generated by tourism activities of this sector is calculated by multiplying the total of tourism expenditures in this sector with the labour coefficient.

The total direct employment by tourism activities is obtained by summing the results of all the sectors.

The intermediate producers serve as input to production directly related to tourism consumption. To define this intermediate production, complex information about the system of intermediate relations between the various sectors of activity is needed.

Variables

The variables depend on the analytical approach chosen. Those mentioned below therefore provide only an overview of the main points which are useful in obtaining good information about the employment situation in the tourism sector. The main variables are :

- Type of activity of the enterprise/local unit of the employee
- Number of employees of the enterprise/local unit
- Number of hours worked
- Structure of the employment : full time/part-time employees, male/female employees, skilled/

unskilled employees, nationality of employees, self employed/employee

— Geographical location of the local unit

— Total number of employees of the local unit/enterprise

— Total labour costs of the local unit/enterprise

— Seasonality

The secondary variables are:

— Age of the employee

— Individual working hours

— Individual working conditions

— Education of the employees

— Position held

— Nature of employment contract

— Salary of the employee

— Structure of the salaries

The above-mentioned variables are either directly or indirectly related; for example, salaries depend on the level of education. It will therefore be necessary to first define the various inter-relations before analysing employment.

Employment variables such as income have to be analysed in conjunction with the number of working hours in order to compare employment figures of the tourism branch with other branches, as the average number of hours worked is normally higher than in other economic activities.

Tourism employment has to be analysed in connection with the supply side of tourism. The requirements of employment statistics must therefore be taken into account in designing supply-side statistics.

It is necessary to analyse both the structure of the education offered for the tourism sector and the needs of the sector, as both unskilled work and highly qualified employment are offered in activities relating to tourism. In order to make comparison of education possible at European level, it is necessary to first analyse the educational needs of the employers and to survey the qualifications and requirements of the employment offered.

Income generated by tourism activity differs greatly from country to country in Europe. Factors to take into account for the income structure are the not very attractive working hours and conditions offered in the tourism sector. These factors must be considered as variables in the context of employment statistics and be taken into account when comparing income generated in the tourism sector with other sectors.

Tourism is a major factor in the economy. The overall income generated by the tourism sector has therefore to be analysed as part of it goes back into private consumption, since changes in tourism employment will influence the demand in other sectors.

Also to be taken into account is the fact that many employees in the tourism sector are foreigners. In many cases a high proportion of their salaries flows back to their country of origin.

This money is an important factor for the respective economy of origin, as it will either be invested or enter the cycle of private consumption.

If employment falls, this will have an impact at both national and international levels, as migrants then flow back and compete again in the employment market of their country of origin.

The general guidelines for collecting data on employment in tourism have been presented in "Statistical units and evaluation approaches" according to the evaluation approach taken. Tax authorities, social insurance authorities, surveys of enterprises, regulatory authorities, labour force surveys and national accounts data are all scurces of information to evaluate employment from the supply side.

From the demand side, detailed tourism expenditure surveys of domestic and inbound (and to a certain extent outbound, e.g. for Travel agencies) visitors would be required to calculate the value of this consumption in terms of employment.

Tourism and the Environment

Environment is defined as the quality of life, living conditions of human beings and the natural environment with suitable habitats for animals and plants. The quality of life is determined by the long-term availability in sufficient quantity and of adequate quality of resources such as water, air, land and space in general as well as raw materials.

The scope of environment statistics includes the media of the natural environment (air/climate, water, land/soil), the biota found within these media, and human settlements. Environment statistics describe the quality and availability of natural resources, human activities and natural events that affect the environment, the impacts of these activities and events and social responses to these impacts.

The environment is a factor influencing tourism demand. Since demand for tourism products is partly determined by the quality of the related environment, the environment can have a positive or negative influence on tourism. Likewise tourism can have a positive and negative impact on the environment.

Already-existing frameworks for environment statistics can be used to identify the topics which are relevant to describing the interrelationship of the environment and tourism.

The UN framework defines four major categories of information relating to the study of the environment:

a. Social and economic activities, natural events

b. Environmental impact of activities

c. Responses to environmental impact

d. Stock, inventories and background conditions

From this framework a selection of topics relevant for a statistical description of the interrelation between tourism and the environment is presented :

Category A, describes different types of impacts on the environment (it is possible to distinguish, through calculations, between impacts caused by tourism and other types of impacts).

Category B, describes changes in the quality of the environment. (these topics are much more difficult to relate to a single cause; information of this type will certainly influence the attraction of a place, and therefore also tourism demand).

Category C, represents information related to actions for environmental protection (it is also of interest as a factor influencing tourism demand)

Category D, includes information about climatic conditions, biological resources and other background conditions.

Supply statistics on accommodation e.g. on occupancy rate for specified periods within the same areas can be used to calculate the number of overnight stays, during the specified period, within a region. It is proposed to use such figures on overnight stays as a basis for calculating the tourism-related share of some types of environmental impacts. This is the case for the amounts of waste generated or the volumes of sewage effluents discharged within an area.

Estimations of the maximum number of overnight stays within a certain region can also be obtained from statistics on tourism supply. This can be of some interest to the local planning authorities, e.g. for calculations of the maximum need for drinking water or decisions concerning the construction and capacity of sewage treatment plants.

The close connection with environment statistics has already been stressed, e.g. for each one of the proposed variables, it is suggested to use the same definitions and classifications as described for the environment. Links also exist between energy and transport statistics.

Since environment statistics include a broad area of subjects, many different methods of data collection are to be used. Already-existing statistics on the environment, transport and energy should be used. The CORINE database of the Statistical Office of the European

Communities can provide useful data concerning the environment.

Combining environment data with tourism demand and supply statistics is important. Another vital issue is the selection of proper emission coefficients. In the following, some recommendations concerning data collection for each one of the proposed main groups of variables are given.

— *Hunting and Fishing*: Information on the participation of visitors could be obtained through household surveys if special questions were included.

— *Energy Use* : The share of transport (by mode) related to tourism can be estimated from data on the mode of transport used and distance travelled provided by tourism demand surveys. These estimates can then be linked to data on passenger transport energy use. Statistics on energy use by establishments for tourist accommodation can only be obtained from enterprise surveys. Statistics on energy use in private vacation dwellings can be calculated if the energy use is regarded as a part of total energy use by private households outside transport.

— *Water Use for Human Consumption* : from statistics on tourism supply, data on the number of overnight stays for a certain period within the region of interest can be obtained and linked to data on water use.

— *Land use and environmental restructuring* : the total area occupied by establishments for tourist accommodation may be estimated from the bed capacity of the various forms of accommodation within a region. An average land use factor per bed for each category of accommodation should be calculated, using existing land or dwelling registers.

— *Waste Loading in Water, Air and Land Statistics*: information on discharge of waste-water broken down by type of treatment can generally be obtained from environment statistics. To calculate the amount of waste-water attributable to tourism, a method using data on number of tourist overnight stays from statistics on tourism supply, comparable to the one described above, may be applied. Statistics on the emissions of various types of air pollutants caused by transport can also be obtained from environment statistics. Statistics on the generation of household wastes can be obtained from environment statistics for most countries.

— *Land Use and Soil quality* : statistics on current land use and on changes in land use can be obtained from environment statistics, but not at a very detailed level.

— *Biological resources* : statistics on population numbers of wild species can only be obtained after special inventories have been made.

— *Water Quality* : statistics on water quality of lakes and rivers are often assembled by local authorities.

— *Climate and air pollution* : Statistics on temperature and precipitation have been produced by the meteorological services for many decades. Measurements on air pollutants in vulnerable built-up areas exist, but as in the case of water quality, the responsibility is with the local authorities, and few examples of good statistical presentation of data can be found.

8

Global Code of Ethics for Tourism

The global Code of Ethic for Tourism sets a frame of reference for the responsible and sustainable development of world tourism at the dawn of the new millennium. It draws inspiration from many similar declarations and industry codes that have come before and it adds new thinking that reflects our changing society at the end of the 20th century. With international tourism forecast to nearly triple in volume over the next 20 years, members of the World Tourism Organization believe that the Global Code of Ethics for Tourism is needed to help minimize the negative impacts of tourism on the environment and on cultural heritage while maximizing the benefits for residents of tourism destinations.

The code was called for in a resolution of the WTO General Assembly meeting in Istanbul in 1997. Over the following two years, a special committee for the preparation of the Global Code of Ethics was formed and a draft document was prepared by the Secretary-General and the legal adviser to WTO in consultation with WTO

Business Council, WTO's Regional Commissions, and the WTO Executive Council.

The United Nations Commission on Sustainable Development meeting in New York in April, 1999 endorsed the concept of the code and requested WTO to seek further input from the private sector, non-governmental organizations and labour organizations. Written comments on the code were received from more than 70 WTO Member States and other entities. The resulting 10 point Global Code of Ethics for Tourism - the culmination of an extensive consultative process- was approved unanimously by the WTO General Assembly meeting in Santiago in October 1999.

The code includes nine articles outlining the "rules of the game" for destinations, governments, tour operators, developers, travel agents, workers and travellers themselves. The tenth article involves the redress of grievances and marks the first time that a code of this type will have a mechanism for enforcement. It will be based on conciliation through the creation of a World Committee on Tourism Ethics made up of representatives of each region of the world and representatives of each group of stakeholders in the tourism sector- governments, the private sector, labour and non-governmental organizations.

The Global Code of Ethics for Tourism, reproduced on the following pages, is intended to be a living documents. Read it. Circulate it widely. Participate in its implementation. Only with your cooperation can we safeguard the future of the tourism industry and expand the sector's contribution to economic prosperity, peace and understanding among all the nations of the world.

Resolution

The General Assembly,

Recalling:

that it had provided at its Istanbul session in 1997 for the formation of a Special Committee for the preparation of the Global Code of Ethics for Tourism and that this Committee met at Cracow, Poland on 7 October 1998, in conjunction with the Quality Support Committee meeting, in order to consider an outline of the said Code,

that based on these initial considerations, the draft Global Code of Ethics for Tourism was prepared by the Secretary-General, with the assistance of the Legal Adviser to WTO and was studied by the WTO Business Council, the Regional Commissions and finally by the Executive Council at its sixtieth session, all of which were invited to formulate their observations,

that the WTO Members were invited to communicate in writing the remarks or suggestions that they could not make at those meetings;

Noting:

that the principle of a Global Code of Ethics for Tourism aroused great interest among the delegations that participated in the seventh session of the Commission on Sustainable Development (CSD) in New York in April 1999,

that after the CSD session, additional consultations were undertaken by the Secretary-General with institutions representative of the tourism industry and the workers, as well as with various non-governmental organizations interested in this process, that, as a result of these discussions and consultations, many written contributions were received by the Secretary-General, which have so far as possible been reflected in the draft submitted to the Assembly for consideration;

Reaffirming that the aim of the Global Code of Ethics for Tourism is to establish a synthesis of the various documents, codes and declarations of the same kind or with comparable aspirations published over the years, to complement them with new considerations reflecting the development of our societies and thus to serve as a frame of reference for the stakeholders in world tourism at the dawn of the next century and millennium,

Adopts the Global Code of Ethics for Tourism, which reads as follows:

We, Members of the World Tourism Organization (WTO) representatives of the world tourism industry, delegates of States, territories, enterprises, institutions and bodies that are), gathered for the General Assembly at Santiago, Chile on this first day of October 1999,

Reasserting the aims set out in Article 3 of the Statutes of the World Tourism Organization, and aware of the "decisive and central" role of this Organization, as recognized by the General Assembly of the United Nations, in promoting and developing tourism with a view to contributing to economic development, international understanding, peace, prosperity and universal respect for, and observance of, human rights and fundamental freedoms for all without distinction as to race, sex, language or religion,

Firmly believing that, through the direct, spontaneous and non-mediatized contacts it engenders between men and women of different cultures and lifestyles, tourism represents a vital force for peace and a factor of friendship and understanding among the peoples of the world,

In keeping with the rationale of reconciling environmental protection, economic development and the fight against poverty in a sustainable manner, as formulated by the United Nations in 1992 at the "Earth Summit" of Rio de Janeiro and expressed in Agenda 21, adopted on that occasion,

Taking into account the swift and continued growth, both past and foreseeable, of the tourism activity, whether for leisure, business, culture, religious or health purposes, and its powerful effects, both positive and negative, on the environment, the economy and the society of both generating and receiving countries, on local communities and indigenous peoples, as well as on international relations and trade,

Aiming to promote responsible, sustainable and universally accessible tourism in the framework of the right of all persons to use their free time for leisure pursuits or travel with respect for the choices of society of all peoples,

But convinced that the world tourism industry as a whole has much to gain by operating in an environment that favours the market economy, private enterprise and free trade and that serves to optimize its beneficial effects on the creation of wealth and employment,

Also firmly convinced that, provided a number of principles and a certain number of rules are observed, responsible and sustainable tourism is by no means incompatible with the growing liberalization of the conditions governing trade in services and under whose aegis the enterprises of this sector operate and that it is possible to reconcile in this sector economy and ecology, environment and development, openness to international trade and protection of social and cultural identities,

Considering that, with such an approach, all the stakeholders in tourism development – national, regional and local administrations, enterprises, business associations, workers in the sector, non-governmental organizations and bodies of all kinds belonging to the tourism industry, as well as host communities, the media and the tourists themselves, have different albeit interdependent responsibilities in the individual and societal development of tourism and that the formulation of their individual rights and duties will contribute to meeting this aim,

Committed, in keeping with the aims pursued by the World Tourism Organization itself since adopting resolution 364(XII) at its General Assembly of 1997 (Istanbul), to promote a genuine partnership between the public and private stakeholders in tourism development, and wishing to see a partnership and cooperation of the same kind extend, in an open and balanced way, to the relations between generating and receiving countries and their respective tourism industries,

Following up on the Manila Declarations of 1980 on World Tourism and of 1997 on the Social Impact of Tourism, as well as on the Tourism Bill of Rights and the Tourist Code adopted at Sofia in 1985 under the aegis of WTO,

But believing that these instruments should be complemented by a set of interdependent principles for their interpretation and application on which the stakeholders in tourism development should model their conduct at the dawn of the twenty-first century,

Using, for the purposes of this instrument, the definitions and classifications applicable to travel, and especially the concepts of "visitor", "tourist" and "tourism", as adopted by the Ottawa International Conference, held from 24 to 28 June 1991 and approved, in 1993, by the United Nations Statistical

Commission at its twenty-seventh session,

Referring in particular to the following instruments:

— Universal Declaration of Human Rights of 10 December 1948;

— International Covenant on Economic, Social and Cultural Rights of 16 December 1966;

— International Covenant on Civil and Political Rights of 16 December 1966;

— Warsaw Convention on Air Transport of 12 October 1929;

— Chicago Convention on International Civil Aviation of 7 December 1944, and the Tokyo, The Hague and Montreal Conventions in relation thereto;

— Convention on Customs Facilities for Tourism of 4 July 1954 and related Protocol;

— Convention concerning the Protection of the World Cultural and Natural Heritage of 23 November 1972;

— Manila Declaration on World Tourism of 10 October 1980;

— Resolution of the Sixth General Assembly of WTO (Sofia) adopting the Tourism Bill of Rights and Tourist Code of 26 September 1985;

— Convention on the Rights of the Child of 26 January 1990;

— Resolution of the Ninth General Assembly of WTO (Buenos Aires) concerning in particular travel facilitation and the safety and security of tourists of 4 October 1991;

— Rio Declaration on the Environment and Development of 13 June 1992;

— General Agreement on Trade in Services of 15 April 1994;

— Convention on Biodiversity of 6 January 1995;

— Resolution of the Eleventh General Assembly of WTO (Cairo) on the prevention of organized sex tourism of 22 October 1995;

— Stockholm Declaration of 28 August 1996 against the Commercial Sexual Exploitation of Children;

— Manila Declaration on the Social Impact of Tourism of 22 May 1997;

Conventions and recommendations adopted by the International Labour Organisation in the area of collective conventions, prohibition of forced labour and child labour, defence of the rights of indigenous peoples, and equal treatment and non-discrimination in the work place; affirm the right to tourism and the freedom of tourist movements, state our wish to promote an equitable, responsible and sustainable world tourism order, whose benefits will be shared by all sectors of society in the context of an open and liberalized international economy, and solemnly adopt to these ends the principles of the Global Code of Ethics for Tourism.

Principles

Article 1: Tourism's contribution to mutual understanding and respect between peoples and societies

The understanding and promotion of the ethical values common to humanity, with an attitude of tolerance and respect for the diversity of religious, philosophical and moral beliefs, are both the foundation and the consequence of responsible tourism; stakeholders in tourism development and tourists themselves should observe the social and cultural traditions and practices of all peoples, including those of minorities and indigenous peoples and to recognize their worth;

Tourism activities should be conducted in harmony with the attributes and traditions of the host regions and countries and in respect for their laws, practices and customs;

The host communities, on the one hand, and local professionals, on the other, should acquaint themselves with and respect the tourists who visit them and find out about their lifestyles, tastes and expectations; the education and training imparted to professionals contribute to a hospitable welcome;

It is the task of the public authorities to provide protection for tourists and visitors and their belongings; they must pay particular attention to the safety of foreign tourists owing to the particular vulnerability they may have; they should facilitate the introduction of specific means of information, prevention, security, insurance and assistance consistent with their needs; any attacks, assaults, kidnappings or threats against tourists or workers in the tourism industry, as well as the wilful destruction of tourism facilities or of elements of cultural or natural heritage should be severely condemned and punished in accordance with their respective national laws;

When travelling, tourists and visitors should not commit any criminal act or any act considered criminal by the laws of the country visited and abstain from any conduct felt to be offensive or injurious by the local populations, or likely to damage the local environment; they should refrain from all trafficking in illicit drugs, arms, antiques, protected species and products and substances that are dangerous or prohibited by national regulations;

Tourists and visitors have the responsibility to acquaint themselves, even before their departure, with the characteristics of the countries they are preparing to visit; they must be aware of the health and security risks inherent in any travel outside their usual environment and behave in such a way as to minimize those risks;

Article 2: Tourism as a vehicle for individual and collective fulfilment

Tourism, the activity most frequently associated with rest and relaxation, sport and access to culture and nature, should be planned and practised as a privileged means of individual and collective fulfilment; when practised with a sufficiently open mind, it is an irreplaceable factor of self-education, mutual tolerance and for learning about the legitimate differences between peoples and cultures and their diversity;

Tourism activities should respect the equality of men and women; they should promote human rights and, more particularly, the individual rights of the most vulnerable groups, notably children, the elderly, the handicapped, ethnic minorities and indigenous peoples;

The exploitation of human beings in any form, particularly sexual, especially when applied to children, conflicts with the fundamental aims of tourism and is the negation of tourism; as such, in accordance with international law, it should be energetically combatted with the cooperation of all the States concerned and penalized without concession by the national legislation of both the countries visited and the countries of the perpetrators of these acts, even when they are carried out abroad;

Travel for purposes of religion, health, education and cultural or linguistic exchanges are particularly beneficial forms of tourism, which deserve encouragement;

The introduction into curricula of education about the value of tourist exchanges, their economic, social and cultural benefits, and also their risks, should be encouraged;

Article 3: Tourism, a factor of sustainable development

All the stakeholders in tourism development should safeguard the natural environment with a view to achieving sound, continuous and sustainable economic growth geared to satisfying equitably the needs and aspirations of present and future generations;

All forms of tourism development that are conducive to saving rare and precious resources, in particular water and energy, as well as avoiding so far as possible waste production, should be given priority and encouraged by national, regional and local public authorities;

The staggering in time and space of tourist and visitor flows, particularly those resulting from paid leave and school holidays, and a more even distribution of holidays should be sought so as to reduce the pressure of tourism activity on the environment and enhance its beneficial impact on the tourism industry and the local economy;

Tourism infrastructure should be designed and tourism activities programmed in such a way as to protect the natural heritage composed of ecosystems and biodiversity and to preserve endangered species of wildlife; the stakeholders in tourism development, and especially professionals, should agree to the imposition of limitations or constraints on their activities when these are exercised in particularly sensitive areas: desert, polar or high mountain regions, coastal areas, tropical forests or wetlands, propitious to the creation of nature reserves or protected areas;

Nature tourism and ecotourism are recognized as being particularly conducive to enriching and enhancing the standing of tourism, provided they respect the natural heritage and local populations and are in keeping with the carrying capacity of the sites;

Article 4: Tourism, a user of the cultural heritage of mankind and contributor to its enhancement

Tourism resources belong to the common heritage of mankind; the communities in whose territories they are situated have particular rights and obligations to them;

Tourism policies and activities should be conducted with respect for the artistic, archaeological and cultural heritage, which they should protect and pass on to future generations; particular care should be devoted to preserving and upgrading monuments, shrines and museums as well as archaeological and historic sites which must be widely open to tourist visits; encouragement should be given to public access to privately-owned cultural property and monuments, with respect for the rights of their owners, as well as to religious buildings, without prejudice to normal needs of worship;

Financial resources derived from visits to cultural sites and monuments should, at least in part, be used for the upkeep, safeguard, development and embellishment of this heritage;

Tourism activity should be planned in such a way as to allow traditional cultural products, crafts and folklore to survive and flourish, rather than causing them to degenerate and become standardized;

Article 5: Tourism, a beneficial activity for host countries and communities

Local populations should be associated with tourism activities and share equitably in the economic, social and cultural benefits they generate, and particularly in the creation of direct and indirect jobs resulting from them;

Tourism policies should be applied in such a way as to help to raise the standard of living of the populations of the regions visited and meet their needs; the planning and architectural approach to and operation of tourism resorts and accommodation should aim to integrate them, to the extent possible, in the local economic and social fabric; where skills are equal, priority should be given to local manpower;

Special attention should be paid to the specific problems of coastal areas and island territories and to vulnerable rural or mountain regions, for which tourism often represents a rare opportunity for development in the face of the decline of traditional economic activities;

Tourism professionals, particularly investors, governed by the regulations laid down by the public authorities, should carry out studies of the impact of their development projects on the environment and natural surroundings; they should also deliver, with the greatest transparency and objectivity, information on their future programmes and their foreseeable repercussions and foster dialogue on their contents with the populations concerned;

Article 6: Obligations of stakeholders in tourism development

Tourism professionals have an obligation to provide tourists with objective and honest information on their places of destination and on the conditions of travel, hospitality and stays; they should ensure that the contractual clauses proposed to their customers are readily understandable as to the nature, price and quality of the services they commit themselves to providing and the financial compensation payable by them in the event of a unilateral breach of contract on their part;

Tourism professionals, insofar as it depends on them, should show concern, in co-operation with the public authorities, for the security and safety, accident prevention, health protection and food safety of those who seek their services; likewise, they should ensure the existence of suitable systems of insurance and assistance; they should accept the reporting obligations prescribed by national regulations and pay fair compensation in the event of failure tc observe their contractual obligations

Tourism professionals, so far as this depends on them, should contribute to the cultural and spiritual fulfilment of tourists and allow them, during their travels, to practise their religions;

The public authorities of the generating States and the host countries, in cooperation with the professionals concerned and their associations, should ensure that the necessary mechanisms are in place for the repatriation of tourists in the event of the bankruptcy of the enterprise that organized their travel;

Governments have the right - and the duty - especially in a crisis, to inform their nationals of the difficult circumstances, or even the dangers they may encounter during their travels abroad; it is their responsibility however to issue such information without prejudicing in an unjustified or exaggerated manner the tourism industry of the host countries and the interests of their own operators; the contents of travel advisories should therefore be discussed beforehand with the authorities of the host countries and the professionals concerned; recommendations formulated should be strictly proportionate to the gravity of the situations encountered and confined to the geographical areas where the insecurity has arisen; such advisories should be qualified or cancelled as soon as a return to normality permits;

The press, and particularly the specialized travel press and the other media, including modern means of electronic communication, should issue honest and balanced information on events and situations that could influence the flow of tourists; they should also provide accurate and reliable information to the consumers of tourism services; the new communication and electronic commerce technologies should also be developed and used for this purpose; as is the case for the media, they should not in any way promote sex tourism;

Article 7: Right to tourism

The prospect of direct and personal access to the discovery and enjoyment of the planet's resources constitutes a right equally open to all the world's inhabitants; the increasingly extensive participation in national and international tourism should be regarded as one of the best possible expressions of the sustained growth of free time, and obstacles should not be placed in its way;

The universal right to tourism must be regarded as the corollary of the right to rest and leisure, including reasonable limitation of working hours and periodic holidays with pay, guaranteed by Article 24 of the Universal Declaration of Human Rights and Article 7.d of the International Covenant on Economic, Social and Cultural Rights;

Social tourism, and in particular associative tourism, which facilitates widespread access to leisure, travel and holidays, should be developed with the support of the public authorities;

Family, youth, student and senior tourism and tourism for people with disabilities, should be encouraged and facilitated;

Article 8: Liberty of tourist movements

Tourists and visitors should benefit, in compliance with international law and national legislation, from the liberty to move within their countries and from one State to another, in accordance with Article 13 of the Universal Declaration of Human Rights; they should have access to places of transit and stay and to tourism and cultural sites without being subject to excessive formalities or discrimination;

Tourists and visitors should have access to all available forms of communication, internal or external; they should benefit from prompt and easy access to local administrative, legal and health services; they should be free to contact the consular representatives of their countries of origin in compliance with the diplomatic conventions in force;

Tourists and visitors should benefit from the same rights as the citizens of the country visited concerning the confidentiality of the personal data and information concerning them, especially when these are stored electronically;

Administrative procedures relating to border crossings whether they fall within the competence of States or result from international agreements, such as visas or health and customs formalities, should be adapted, so far as possible, so as to facilitate to the maximum freedom of travel and widespread access to international tourism; agreements between groups of countries to harmonize and simplify these procedures should be encouraged; specific taxes and levies penalizing the tourism industry and undermining its competitiveness should be gradually phased out or corrected;

So far as the economic situation of the countries from which they come permits, travellers should have access to allowances of convertible currencies needed for their travels;

Article 9: Rights of the workers and entrepreneurs in the tourism industry

The fundamental rights of salaried and self-employed workers in the tourism industry and related activities, should be guaranteed under the supervision of the national and local administrations, both of their States of origin and of the host countries with particular care, given the specific constraints linked in particular to the seasonality of their activity, the global dimension of their industry and the flexibility often required of them by the nature of their work;

Salaried and self-employed workers in the tourism industry and related activities have the right and the duty to acquire appropriate initial and continuous training; they should be given adequate social protection; job insecurity should be limited so far as possible; and a specific status, with particular regard to their social welfare, should be offered to seasonal workers in the sector;

Any natural or legal person, provided he, she or it has the necessary abilities and skills, should be entitled to develop a professional activity in the field of tourism under existing national laws; entrepreneurs and investors - especially in the area of small and medium-sized enterprises - should be entitled to free access to the tourism sector with a minimum of legal or administrative restrictions;

Exchanges of experience offered to executives and workers, whether salaried or not, from different countries, contributes to foster the development of the world tourism industry; these movements should be facilitated so far as possible in compliance with the applicable national laws and international conventions;

As an irreplaceable factor of solidarity in the development and dynamic growth of international exchanges, multinational enterprises of the tourism industry should not exploit the dominant positions they sometimes occupy; they should avoid becoming the vehicles of cultural and social models artificially imposed on the host communities; in exchange for their freedom to invest and trade which should be fully recognized, they should involve themselves in local development, avoiding, by the excessive repatriation of their profits or their induced imports, a reduction of their contribution to the economies in which they are established;

Partnership and the establishment of balanced relations between enterprises of generating and receiving countries contribute to the sustainable development of tourism and an equitable distribution of the benefits of its growth;

Article 10: Implementation of the principles of the Global Code of Ethics for Tourism

The public and private stakeholders in tourism development should cooperate in the implementation of these principles and monitor their effective application;

The stakeholders in tourism development should recognize the role of international institutions, among which the World Tourism Organization ranks first, and non-governmental organizations with competence in the field of tourism promotion and development, the protection of human rights, the environment or health, with due respect for the general principles of international law;

The same stakeholders should demonstrate their intention to refer any disputes concerning the application or interpretation of the Global Code of Ethics for Tourism for conciliation to an impartial third body known as the World Committee on Tourism Ethics.

Draft Protocol of Implementation

I. Body responsible for interpreting, applying and evaluating the provisions of the Global Code of Ethics for Tourism

(a) A World Committee on Tourism Ethics shall be created comprising twelve eminent persons independent of governments and twelve alternates, selected on the basis of their competence in the field of tourism and related fields; they shall not receive any orders or instructions from those who proposed their nomination or who designated them and shall not report to them.

(b) The members of the World Committee on Tourism Ethics shall be appointed as follows:

— six members and six alternate members designated by the WTO Regional Commissions, on the proposal of the States Members of WTO;

— a member and an alternate designated by the autonomous territories that are Associate Members of WTO from among their members;

— four members and four alternate members elected by the WTO General Assembly from among the Affiliate Members of WTO representing professionals or employees of the tourism industry, universities and non-governmental organizations, after conferring with the Committee of Affiliate Members;

— a chairman, who may be an eminent person not belonging to WTO, elected by the other members of the Committee, on the proposal of the Secretary-General of WTO.

The Legal Adviser of the World Tourism Organization shall participate, when necessary, and in an advisory capacity, in the Committee meetings; the Secretary-General shall attend ex officio or may arrange to be represented at its meetings.

On appointing the members of the Committee, account shall be taken of the need for a balanced geographical composition of this body and for a diversification of the qualifications and personal status of its members, from both the economic and social as well as the legal viewpoint; the members shall be appointed for four years and their term of office may be renewed only once; in the event of a vacancy, the member shall be replaced by his alternate, it being understood that if the vacancy concerns both the member and his alternate, the Committee itself shall fill the vacant seat; if the

Chairman's seat is vacant he or she shall be replaced in the conditions set out above.

(c) The WTO Regional Commissions shall act, in the cases provided for in paragraphs I(d), (g) and (h), as well as II(a), (b), (f) and (g) below of this Protocol, as regional committees on tourism ethics.

(d) The World Committee on Tourism Ethics shall establish its own Rules of Procedure, which shall apply equally, mutatis mutandis, to the Regional Commissions when these are acting as regional committees on tourism ethics; the presence of two-thirds of the Committee members shall be necessary to constitute a quorum at its meetings; in the event that a member is absent, he may be replaced by his alternate; in the event of a tie in the voting, the chairman shall have the casting vote.

(e) When proposing the candidature of an eminent person to serve on the Committee, each Member of WTO shall undertake to cover the travel expenses and daily subsistence allowances occasioned by the participation in the meetings of the person whose nomination it has proposed, it being understood that the members of the Committee shall not receive any remuneration; the expenses incurred by the participation of the Chairman of the Committee, also unremunerated, may be borne by the WTO budget; the secretariat of the Committee shall be provided by the services of WTO; the operating costs remaining payable by the Organization may, wholly or in part, be charged to a trust fund financed by voluntary contributions.

(f) The World Committee on Tourism Ethics shall meet in principle once a year; whenever a dispute is referred to it for settlement, the chairman shall consult the other members and the Secretary-General of WTO about the expediency of convening an extraordinary meeting.

(g) The functions of the World Committee on Tourism Ethics and the WTO Regional Commissions shall be the evaluation of the implementation of this Code and conciliation; it may invite experts or external institutions to contribute to its proceedings.

(h) On the basis of periodic reports submitted to them by Full Members, Associate Members and Affiliate Members of WTO, the WTO Regional Commissions shall, every two years, as regional committees on tourism ethics, examine the application of the Code in their respective regions; they shall record their findings in a report to the World Committee on Tourism Ethics; the reports of the Regional Commissions may contain suggestions to amend or supplement the Global Code of Ethics for Tourism.

(i) The World Committee on Tourism Ethics shall exercise a global function as a "watchdog" for the problems encountered in implementing the Code and for the proposed solutions; it shall summarize the reports drawn up by the Regional Commissions and supplement them with the information it has collected with the assistance of the Secretary-General and the support of the Committee of Affiliate Members, which shall include, should the need arise, proposals to amend or supplement the Global Code of Ethics for Tourism.

(j) The Secretary-General shall refer the report of the World Committee on Tourism Ethics to the Executive Council, together with his own observations, for consideration and transmission to the General Assembly with the Council's recommendations; the General Assembly shall decide what follow-up action to take on the report and the recommendations thus submitted to it, which the national tourism administrations and other stakeholders in tourism development shall subsequently have the task of implementing.

II. Conciliation mechanism for the settlement of disputes

(a) In the event of a dispute concerning the interpretation or application of the Global Code of Ethics for Tourism, two or more stakeholders in tourism development may jointly refer it to the World Committee on Tourism Ethics; if the dispute is between two or more stakeholders belonging to the same region, the Parties should refer the matter to the competent WTO Regional Commission in its capacity as a regional committee on tourism ethics.

(b) The States, as well as tourism enterprises and bodies, may declare that they accept in advance the competence of the World Committee on Tourism Ethics or of a WTO Regional Commission for any dispute concerning the interpretation or application of this Code, or for certain categories of dispute; in this case, the Committee or the competent Regional Commission shall be considered as validly referred to unilaterally by the other Party to the dispute.

(c) When a dispute is submitted in the first instance to the World Committee on Tourism Ethics for consideration, its chairman shall appoint a sub-committee of three members who shall be responsible for examining the dispute.

(d) The World Committee on Tourism Ethics to which a dispute has been referred shall reach a decision on the basis of the record drawn up by the Parties to the dispute; the Committee may ask these Parties for additional information and, if deemed useful, may hear them at their request; the expenses incurred by this hearing shall be borne by the Parties unless the circumstances are considered exceptional by the Committee; the failure of one of the Parties to appear even though he or she has been given a reasonable opportunity to participate, shall not prevent the Committee from making a ruling.

(e) Unless otherwise agreed by the Parties, the World Committee on Tourism Ethics shall announce its decision within three months of the date on which it was referred to; it shall present recommendations to the Parties suitable to form the basis of a settlement; the Parties shall immediately inform the chairman of the Committee that has examined the dispute of the action they have taken on these recommendations.

(f) If a dispute is referred to a WTO Regional Commission, it shall announce its decision following the same procedure, mutatis mutandis, as that applied by the World Committee on Tourism Ethics when it intervenes in the first instance.

(g) If within a period of two months after notification of the proposals of the Committee or of a Regional Commission the Parties have failed to agree on the terms of a final settlement, the Parties or one of them may refer the dispute to a plenary session of the World Committee on Tourism Ethics; when the Committee has made a ruling in the first instance, the members that served on the sub-committee that examined the dispute may not take part in this plenary session and shall be replaced by their alternates; if these intervened in the first instance, the members shall not be prevented from participating.

(h) The plenary session of the World Committee on Tourism Ethics shall make its ruling following the procedure laid out in paragraphs II(d) and (e) above; if no solution has been found at a previous stage, it shall formulate final conclusions for the settlement of the dispute, which the Parties, if they agree with their contents, will be recommended to apply at the earliest possible opportunity; these conclusions shall be made public, even if the process of conciliation has not been successfully completed and one of the Parties refuses to accept the final conclusions proposed.

(i) Full Members, Associate Members and Affiliate Members of WTO, as well as States that are not members of WTO, may declare that they accept in advance as binding and, where applicable, subject to the sole reservation of reciprocity, the final conclusions of the World Committee on Tourism Ethics in the disputes, or in a private dispute to which they are party.

(j) Likewise, the States may accept as binding or subject to exequatur the final conclusions of the World Committee on Tourism Ethics in disputes to which their nationals are party or which should be applied in their territory.

(k) Tourism enterprises and bodies may include in their contractual documents a provision making the final conclusions of the World Committee on Tourism Ethics binding in their relations with their contracting parties.

Bibliography

Eagles, P., "Key Issues in Ecotourism Management", *Paper presented at the Western Australia Annual Tourism Conference*, Perth, 1995.

Jenner, P., and Smith, C., "The Adventure Travel Market in Europe", *Travel and Tourism Analyst*, No.4, 1999.

Hoekman, B., "*Towards a more Balanced and Comprehensive Services Agreement*, 1999.

Honey, M., *Ecotourism and Sustainable Development; Who Owns Paradise?*, 1999.

Mashayekhi M., "General Agreement on Trade in services", *TWN Seminar of Current Issues on Trade, the WTO and the Developing Countries*, Geneva, 29-30 April 1998.

UNCTAD, "Series on Issues in Competition Law and Policies", *Recent Developments in Trade and Competition Issues in the Services Sector: A Review Of Practices in Travel and Tourism*, 1999.

UNCTAD, "International Trade in Tourism-Related Services: Issues and Options for Developing Countries", *Background note by the Secretariat*, TD/B/COM.1/EM.6/2, 8 April 1998

Vellas F., and Becherel L, *International Tourism*, Macmillan Press Ltd, 1995.

World Tourism Organisation, (WTO/OMT), *Tourism and the General Agreement on Trade in Services*, Madrid, in collaboration with GATT and UNCTAD, 1994.

_____________, *Report of the Seminar on GATS Implications for Tourism*, World Tourism Organisation Seminar and Conference Proceedings, Milan, 2-3 December 1995.

_____________, "Tourism 2020 Vision East Asia and Pacific", *Volume 3*, WTO, Madrid, Spain, 2000.

Index